I0152565

You Are God's Beloved Children

Independently Published
Fort Lauderdale, Florida
https://amazon.com/author/woodyclermont

You Are God's Beloved Children

Surviving the Furnace of Affliction

Woody R. Clermont

First Edition
August 30, 2025

© 2025 Woody R. Clermont. All rights reserved.

No part of this publication may be reproduced, distributed, or transmitted in any form or by any means, including photocopying, recording, or other electronic or mechanical methods, without the prior written permission of the publisher, except in the case of brief quotations embodied in critical reviews and certain other noncommercial uses permitted by copyright law. For permission requests, write to wclermont2004@gmail.com.

Legal and Tax Disclaimer: This book is for educational and informational purposes only. It does not constitute legal, tax, accounting, or financial advice, and no attorney–client or other professional relationship is created by reading it. Trust and estate laws vary by state and change over time; consult a qualified attorney and tax professional in your jurisdiction before taking action. The author and publisher disclaim any liability for actions taken or not taken based on this work.

Trademarks: Product and company names mentioned herein may be trademarks of their respective owners. Use of such names is for identification only and does not imply endorsement.

ISBNs:
Paperback: 979-8-9993281-7-5

Library of Congress Control Number (LCCN): LCCN Pending

Cover design: The Unrelenting Alchemist
Interior design: W.R. Clermont

Printed in the United States of America

Independently Published, Fort Lauderdale, Florida

"I still believe that standing up for the truth of God is the greatest thing in the world. This is the end of life. The end of life is not to be happy. The end of life is not to achieve pleasure and avoid pain. The end of life is to do the will of God, come what may."
— **Reverend Doctor Martin Luther King, Jr.**

"The punishment of the wicked as well as the reward of the righteous is consequential, that is to say, it grows out of the nature of the life lived here. The development of spiritual capacity here through adherence to the principles of Jesus Christ, which involves the highest spiritual and ethical ideals and values, gives ability to enjoy spiritual blessedness in the future life... I believe in future reward and in future punishment, each consequent upon the life lived here and absolutely determined by that life. We carry with us the capacity for bliss or the instruments of our own punishment."
— **Reverend Edgar Amos Love.**

Acknowledgments

Thank you to the people who made this book possible: You know who you are. Thank you to the Most High God, above all others. Thank you to my Lord and Savior, Jesus Christ. Thank you to the Holy Spirit of this Universe.

Permissions and Requests

To request permission to quote, reproduce charts or checklists, or adapt materials from this book, please email wclermont2004@gmail.com. For speaking, bulk orders, or instructor copies, visit https://amazon.com/author/woodyclermont.

ISBN 979-8-9993281-7-5

9 798999 328175

Preface

This book began with a scriptural jolt: *"I said, you are gods"* (Ps. 82:6), a line Jesus Himself quotes (John 10:34), standing alongside the first truth spoken over humanity: *"God created man in His own image"* (Gen. 1:27). What does it mean to bear the image of God—and why would Jesus point us back to that daring claim? Not to inflate our egos, but to awaken our calling. We were made to reflect God's character in the world: His holiness, mercy, justice, truth, and love.

You Are God's Beloved Children is not an invitation to self-deification. It is a summons to Christ-shaped dignity and responsibility. Psalm 82 rebukes unjust rulers who forgot God's ways; Jesus' citation exposes our small views of God and ourselves. The gospel answers both: in Christ we are adopted as sons and daughters (John 1:12; Rom. 8:15–17) and called to share, by grace, in His life (*"partakers of the divine nature,"* 2 Pet. 1:4). This is not about grasping at divinity, but receiving new life from the Living God.

These pages pursue a simple pattern: Scripture first,

then reflection, then practice. Each chapter traces a facet of image-bearing—identity, prayer, justice, humility, authority, holiness, resurrection hope—and presses it into daily life. You will find questions for the heart, habits for the week, and words to pray. Formation requires more than admiration; it asks for apprenticeship to Jesus. The aim is not spiritual novelty but faithful recovery: Word and prayer, worship and fellowship, generosity and service—the ordinary means by which God makes people new.

The title is bold; the way is lowly. Christ shows us that true greatness kneels to wash feet, carries the cross before wearing a crown, and loves enemies while praying for their good. If we are to reflect God, we must look long at Jesus. In Him the image is unbroken, the Father is made known, and our future is already alive.

I write with gratitude for the church that taught me the creed, the Scriptures that read me as I read them, and the Spirit who convicts, comforts, and conforms us to Christ. My hope is modest and immense at once: that as you read you will hear the Father's voice naming you *beloved*, the Son's call to follow, and the Spirit's nudge toward concrete obedience today.

May this book steady your steps and lift your eyes. May it remind you that your life is not small: you bear the image of the King. And may the Lord teach us, in every ordinary place, to live as His likeness for the life of the world.

"Thy kingdom come, Thy will be done, on earth as it is in heaven." (Matt. 6:10)

— Woody R. Clermont

Contents

Contents

Chapter 1

In the Image of God

Scripture Foundation

"So God created man in his own image, in the image of God he created him; male and female he created them." (Genesis 1:27)
"I said, 'You are gods; you are all sons of the Most High."' (Psalm 82:6)
"Jesus answered them, 'Is it not written in your Law, "I said, you are gods"?"' (John 10:34)

Introduction: The Mystery of the Image

From the first chapter of Genesis, Scripture declares that humanity was created with a unique dignity: we are

made in the image and likeness of God. Unlike the rest
of creation, which came forth by divine command,
humanity was personally formed and stamped with
God's imprint. This doctrine, often called the *imago Dei*,
has been the foundation of Christian understanding of
human worth, identity, and vocation. It tells us that
every man and woman carries inherent dignity, not
earned by achievement but given by creation.

Yet this truth is more than an abstract theological claim.
It is the bedrock of ethics, justice, community, and
discipleship. Psalm 82 pushes this reality further by
reminding us that those entrusted with bearing God's
image are accountable to live in accordance with His
character. Jesus Himself, centuries later, quotes this
psalm in defense of His own mission and identity, calling
His hearers to a higher vision of who they truly are.

Genesis 1:27 — The Beginning of Identity

Genesis 1:27 stands as a crown jewel in the creation
narrative. In a world where people often defined
themselves by tribe, occupation, or social status, this
verse declares something revolutionary: all humanity,
male and female alike, reflects the Creator. The phrase
"image of God" is not about physical resemblance but
spiritual representation. To be made in God's image is to
share in attributes such as rationality, creativity, moral
awareness, relational capacity, and spiritual longing.

The imago Dei gives humanity a unique vocation:

stewardship over creation (Gen. 1:28). Dominion is not exploitation but faithful caretaking, modeling God's own governance, which is wise, loving, and just. When we cultivate the earth, create art, form families, establish communities, and act with compassion, we mirror the God who created us.

Psalm 82:6 — A Sobering Reminder

Psalm 82 is a striking passage. God stands in judgment over the "gods" — whether human rulers or spiritual beings — and rebukes them for injustice and oppression. In verse 6 He says, "I said, you are gods; you are all sons of the Most High." The phrase acknowledges the divine imprint within humanity but confronts the misuse of that dignity. Those who were meant to reflect God's justice have instead exploited the weak, favored the wicked, and perverted righteousness.

The psalm warns that carrying God's image is not merely an honor but a responsibility. To bear His likeness while acting unjustly is to live in contradiction. Thus, the divine title "sons of the Most High" becomes a call to accountability: to act as true representatives of God's character on earth.

John 10:34 — Jesus' Bold Application

In John 10, Jesus is accused of blasphemy for calling Himself the Son of God. His reply is brilliant: He cites Psalm 82:6. If Scripture itself declares, "You are gods," then how can His own claim of being God's Son be dismissed so quickly? His argument is not merely rhetorical; it reveals the depth of the imago Dei. Humanity was created with divine imprint, and yet the fullness of that identity is revealed only in Christ, the perfect image of the invisible God (Col. 1:15).

By using Psalm 82, Jesus both defends His identity and confronts His opponents with their own. They accuse Him while forgetting that their own Scriptures testify to the divine dignity of humanity. Jesus' words serve as an invitation to see themselves—and Him—through the lens of God's purposes.

Theological Implications of the Imago Dei

The doctrine of the imago Dei shapes nearly every aspect of Christian life and theology:

- **Human Dignity:** Every person, regardless of age, ability, ethnicity, or status, possesses inherent worth because of God's image. This undergirds Christian views on justice, equality, and care for the vulnerable.

- **Human Responsibility:** Image-bearing means we are called to live in holiness, justice, and love, reflecting God's nature in our daily lives.

- **Christ as Fulfillment:** While sin distorts the image, Christ restores it. Believers are being conformed to His likeness through the Spirit (2 Cor. 3:18).

- **Community and Relationship:** Since both male and female were created in God's image, relationships between men and women are meant to reflect equality, mutual honor, and cooperation in God's mission.

- **Vocation and Work:** Our labor—whether building, teaching, parenting, or governing—participates in God's ongoing work of sustaining and redeeming creation.

Practical Applications

How does this truth shape everyday Christian living? If being made in the image of God is not simply an abstract idea but the very bedrock of our identity, then it must shape every sphere of life. The imago Dei is not a doctrine to admire from a distance; it is a truth to embody in daily rhythms, relationships, decisions, and worship. Below are five core areas where this reality reshapes how we live, each flowing from Genesis 1:27, illuminated by Psalm 82, and fulfilled in Christ.

1. Personal Identity

From the beginning, Scripture anchors our worth in God's creative act: "So God created man in his own image." (Gen. 1:27). This means identity is not earned through accomplishment, possessions, status, or approval. Our identity is not fragile, built on shifting cultural standards, but firm, grounded in divine declaration.

In a world obsessed with self-definition—whether through career, achievement, appearance, or even failure—the Christian rests in the identity already bestowed by God. To know we are image-bearers frees us from the exhausting cycle of proving ourselves. Paul reminds us in Ephesians 2:10 that "we are God's workmanship, created in Christ Jesus to do good works." We are not accidents of biology or fate; we are intentional creations with eternal worth.

This truth reshapes how we respond to shame. Sin distorts the image but does not erase it. Though we all "fall short of the glory of God" (Rom. 3:23), Christ restores what sin has marred. Baptism, union with Christ, and the indwelling Spirit renew the image daily. Thus, we need not be defined by our past sins, failures, or the voices of condemnation. Instead, we live out of God's word over us: beloved, chosen, redeemed.

Practically, this calls us to rehearse identity daily through Scripture meditation, confession of faith, and resistance of lies. A believer might begin the day by reciting: "I am created in God's image, redeemed by Christ's blood, and sealed by the Spirit. Nothing can separate me from His love" (Rom. 8:39). Such repetition is not empty ritual but spiritual warfare against false identities that enslave.

2. Relationships

If every person carries the divine imprint, then our relationships are transformed. The command to "love your neighbor as yourself" (Mark 12:31) is not an abstract ideal; it is rooted in the imago Dei. To dishonor another is to dishonor God's likeness in them. Gossip, prejudice, exploitation, and abuse are not merely social wrongs but theological contradictions: they strike at the reflection of God.

Consider James 3:9–10: "With the tongue we bless our Lord and Father, and with it we curse people who are made in the likeness of God. From the same mouth come blessing and cursing. My brothers, these things ought not to be so." The apostle reminds us that speech against others is speech against God's image. Thus, respect, patience, forgiveness, and compassion are not optional but essential marks of discipleship.

Marriage itself flows from this truth: male and female created in God's image, designed to reflect His covenant faithfulness (Eph. 5:22–33). Parenting echoes it as well: children are arrows crafted in God's likeness, entrusted to parents for training in righteousness (Ps. 127:3–5; Prov. 22:6). Friendships too bear the weight of this doctrine: Christian fellowship is not utilitarian but sacramental—through the face of the other we glimpse the face of God.

Practically, this reshapes conflict. Instead of viewing the "other" as an enemy, we see them as an image-bearer. This does not excuse sin or injustice but frames confrontation in dignity. Forgiveness becomes possible, not because the wrong was light, but because the offender is still stamped with divine likeness.

3. Justice and Mercy

Psalm 82 directly links the imago Dei with accountability for justice: "Give justice to the weak and the fatherless; maintain the right of the afflicted and the destitute" (vv. 3–4). Those who bear God's image are entrusted to reflect His justice. When rulers, judges, or communities exploit the vulnerable, they betray their calling. God Himself rises to judge them for failing to live as true image-bearers.

Justice, then, is not an optional add-on to Christian life. It is central to our vocation. Micah 6:8 summarizes: "What does the Lord require of you but to do justice, to love mercy, and to walk humbly with your God?" The imago Dei requires us to treat the poor, the immigrant, the orphan, and the widow with dignity. When we act justly, we echo God's character; when we ignore injustice, we deny His likeness in us.

Mercy, equally, flows from the image. God is "merciful and gracious, slow to anger and abounding in steadfast love" (Ps. 103:8). To reflect His image means we extend compassion even when it is costly. Jesus commands, "Be merciful, even as your Father is merciful" (Luke 6:36). Mercy is not weakness but divine strength displayed in patience, forgiveness, and generosity.

Practically, this means Christians cannot separate piety from justice. Church attendance without care for the oppressed is hypocrisy (Isa. 1:13–17). Faithful image-bearing leads believers to defend the unborn, care for the elderly, oppose racial injustice, support the poor, and embody mercy in daily interactions. It also means examining personal habits: how do my spending, my words, my votes, and my silence reflect or distort God's justice?

4. Discipleship

Discipleship is the process of being restored to the true image of God in Christ. Genesis 1 tells us who we are; the Gospels show us who we are meant to become. Jesus, "the image of the invisible God" (Col. 1:15), models perfect humanity. To follow Him is to learn His ways until His life is reflected in ours.

Discipleship is not merely intellectual assent or doctrinal mastery. It is apprenticeship. Jesus calls His followers not to admire Him from afar but to "take up [their] cross daily" (Luke 9:23) and imitate His humility (Phil. 2:5–8). As disciples walk with Him, they are conformed to His likeness (Rom. 8:29). This process is lifelong, involving Scripture study, prayer, fellowship, sacraments, and obedience.

The image of God in us is like a mirror tarnished by sin. Discipleship is the Spirit's ongoing polishing work, restoring the mirror until it reflects Christ clearly. Paul writes in 2 Corinthians 3:18, "We all, with unveiled faces, beholding the glory of the Lord, are being transformed into the same image from one degree of glory to another." This is discipleship: progressive transformation into Christ's likeness.

Practically, discipleship requires intentional rhythms: daily Scripture, prayer, confession, fasting, service, and community accountability. It also requires embracing suffering as formative, trusting that God uses trials to shape us into Christ's image (James 1:2–4). Every act of obedience, no matter how small, is a stroke of restoration on the canvas of the imago Dei.

5. Worship

Finally, worship is the ultimate expression of image-bearing. Humanity was created to reflect God's glory back to Him. To worship is to align with our true purpose. Romans 12:1 describes worship as offering our bodies as living sacrifices, holy and pleasing to God. This is not limited to singing hymns but encompasses all of life: work, relationships, leisure, and service can all become acts of worship.

In Revelation, the vision of heaven is filled with worshippers from every tribe and tongue proclaiming God's glory (Rev. 7:9–12). This is the destiny of image-bearers: restored, redeemed, and gathered in unbroken praise. Every act of worship now anticipates that eternal future.

Worship also heals distortion. Where sin teaches us to

glorify self, worship redirects glory to God. Where fear and despair threaten to eclipse hope, worship reorients us to God's sovereignty and love. In worship we are reminded of our identity: not consumers, not slaves, not failures—but children of the Most High who exist to delight in Him.

Practically, this means participating in both corporate and private worship. Corporate worship through Word, sacrament, prayer, and song trains our hearts together as the Body of Christ. Private worship through Scripture reading, prayer, journaling, and even song at home nurtures daily communion. Together, they shape us into true reflections of God's glory.

Summary

The imago Dei is not a distant doctrine but a living reality. It grounds our personal identity, transforms our relationships, demands justice and mercy, shapes discipleship, and culminates in worship. To bear God's image is to live every moment aware that we are mirrors of the divine—broken but being restored, finite yet made for eternity, ordinary yet stamped with glory.

A Christ-Centered Vision of the Image

Jesus Christ is described as the "exact representation" of God's being (Heb. 1:3). He is not merely another prophet pointing the way toward God; He is God made visible, the Word made flesh (John 1:14). In Him we see what it means to live fully in the image of God: truth without compromise, mercy without weakness, holiness without arrogance, and love without limit. Christ embodies the imago Dei in its fullness, showing us both the perfection of God and the pattern for humanity.

When we look at Jesus, we see the restoration of Eden's vision. Adam was called to bear God's image but fell into rebellion, distorting that likeness. Christ is called the "last Adam" (1 Cor. 15:45), who succeeds where the first Adam failed. He lives in perfect obedience to the Father, resists temptation, and models the harmony of divine will and human action. His miracles reveal the compassion of God's image at work—healing the sick, feeding the hungry, forgiving the sinful, and embracing the marginalized. His teaching embodies wisdom and justice, restoring people to their true dignity. His death demonstrates self-giving love at its highest, and His resurrection unveils the destiny of image-bearers: life everlasting.

As we follow Him, we are not just reminded of who we were created to be—we are actively being transformed into His likeness. The Spirit's work is to conform us to Christ (Rom. 8:29), polishing the tarnished mirror of the imago Dei until we shine with the reflected glory of the Lord (2 Cor. 3:18). This transformation is ongoing, gradual, and at times painful, but it is sure. What was fractured in Eden is being mended in the body of Christ.

Thus, the imago Dei is not static; it is dynamic. It began in Eden as humanity's original glory, was marred by the Fall through sin and rebellion, is restored in Christ through the cross and resurrection, and will be perfected in the resurrection when we see Him as He is (1 John 3:2). On that day, the process of sanctification will be complete, and the image will no longer be distorted by sin, weakness, or death. We will bear, fully and forever, the likeness of the heavenly Man (1 Cor. 15:49). This vision of Christ-centered restoration gives believers unshakable hope: what God began in creation and renewed in Christ He will bring to completion in glory (Phil. 1:6).

Extended Reflection Questions

- How does understanding yourself as made in God's image change the way you view your past failures and future potential? Does it free you from shame and open you to hope?

- In what ways might you be tempted to misuse the dignity of God's image for self-centered gain—whether in pride, exploitation, or neglect of others?

- Where do you see Christ restoring the image of God in your own life through transformation, healing, or growth? Can you name specific habits or graces that mark His work?

- How does the imago Dei shape your view of social issues such as poverty, racism, injustice, or the treatment of the unborn and elderly? How might seeing others as God's image-bearers reshape your posture toward them?

- What practices—prayer, Scripture meditation, fasting, confession, acts of service—help you live more fully as an image-bearer of God? Which of these do you feel called to strengthen in your life right now?

- How does corporate worship and life in the church help you live out the imago Dei more faithfully than you could alone?

- In what ways does Jesus' example—His truthfulness, His mercy, His humility, His love—challenge your own reflection of God's image?

- How might a deeper grasp of the imago Dei change the way you parent, mentor, or disciple others in their walk with Christ?

Conclusion

The opening chapter of Genesis, the prophetic rebuke of Psalm 82, and the bold defense of Jesus in John 10 converge on one great truth: humanity was created to reflect the living God. This identity is both a staggering gift and a solemn calling. We are not accidents of history, nor products of chance; we are sons and daughters of the Most High, stamped with His likeness and invited into fellowship with Him. To live in this truth is to embrace both dignity and responsibility: to reflect God's holiness in our moral lives, to embody His compassion in our dealings with others, and to pursue His justice in a world scarred by oppression and sin.

Yet we must also recognize the tension: the image is real,

but it has been marred by sin. Left to ourselves, we distort rather than display the divine likeness. But in Christ, the perfect Image, we find both our example and our redemption. His life shows us what humanity was meant to be; His cross reconciles what humanity broke; His resurrection guarantees the renewal of the image in us. In Him, the Spirit works daily to restore what was lost, polishing the mirror of our souls until we shine again with God's glory.

Therefore, to bear the image of God is not only to carry dignity but to live in continual transformation. We are invited to walk in the Spirit, to put on the new self "created after the likeness of God in true righteousness and holiness" (Eph. 4:24). We are called to live not for self, but for the God whose image we bear, reflecting His character into every corner of creation. And we are promised that one day, when Christ appears, the work will be finished—we shall see Him as He is, and we shall be like Him (1 John 3:2).

In the end, the imago Dei is a reminder of our origin, a summons to responsibility in the present, and a promise of glory in the future. Through Christ, we become what we were always meant to be: true reflections of the God who made us, radiating His light into the world until the day we are fully remade in His presence forever.

Chapter 2

Sons and Daughters of the Most High

Scripture Foundation

"The Spirit himself testifies with our spirit that we are God's children. Now if we are children, then we are heirs—heirs of God and co-heirs with Christ, if indeed we share in his sufferings in order that we may also share in his glory." (Romans 8:16–17)

"See what great love the Father has lavished on us, that we should be called children of God! And that is what we are! The reason the world does not know us is that it did not know him." (1 John 3:1)

"But to all who did receive him, who believed in his name,

he gave the right to become children of God." (John 1:12)

"Because you are his sons, God sent the Spirit of his Son into our hearts, the Spirit who calls out, 'Abba, Father.' So you are no longer a slave, but God's child; and since you are his child, God has made you also an heir." (Galatians 4:6–7)

"The Spirit you received does not make you slaves, so that you live in fear again; rather, the Spirit you received brought about your adoption to sonship. And by him we cry, 'Abba, Father.'" (Romans 8:15)

"I will be a Father to you, and you shall be my sons and daughters, says the Lord Almighty." (2 Corinthians 6:18)

"The Lord disciplines the one he loves, and he chastens everyone he accepts as his son." (Hebrews 12:6)

"For you are all sons of God through faith in Christ Jesus. For all of you who were baptized into Christ have clothed yourselves with Christ." (Galatians 3:26–27)

"For the creation waits in eager expectation for the children of God to be revealed." (Romans 8:19)

"Blessed are the peacemakers, for they shall be called sons of God." (Matthew 5:9)

"In love he predestined us for adoption to sonship through Jesus Christ, in accordance with his pleasure and will—to the praise of his glorious grace." (Ephesians 1:4–6)

"And I will be your Father, and you will be my sons and

daughters, says the Lord Almighty.” (2 Samuel 7:14, echoed in 2 Corinthians 6:18)

“For everyone who is led by the Spirit of God is a son of God.” (Romans 8:14)

“The Spirit you received brought about your adoption to sonship.” (Romans 8:15) — a reminder repeated for emphasis in Paul's teaching.

“For the Lord your God is God of gods and Lord of lords, the great God, mighty and awesome, who shows no partiality and accepts no bribes. He defends the cause of the fatherless and the widow, and loves the foreigner residing among you, giving them food and clothing.” (Deuteronomy 10:17–18) — God reveals His Fatherly nature even in the Old Testament by defending the orphan.

“As a father has compassion on his children, so the Lord has compassion on those who fear him.” (Psalm 103:13)

“Do everything without grumbling or arguing, so that you may become blameless and pure, children of God without fault in a warped and crooked generation. Then you will shine among them like stars in the sky.” (Philippians 2:14–15)

“For you did not receive a spirit that makes you a slave again to fear, but you received the Spirit of adoption as sons, by whom we cry, Abba! Father!” (Romans 8:15, ESV) — a theme central to Paul's gospel.

"The Lord Almighty says: I will be a Father to you, and you shall be sons and daughters to me." (2 Corinthians 6:18, quoting Old Testament covenant promises)

"All who are victorious will inherit all this, and I will be their God and they will be my children." (Revelation 21:7)

Taken together, these passages weave a consistent and powerful testimony across the canon of Scripture: God is not content for us to remain distant creatures or wandering servants—He draws us near as sons and daughters. From His covenant promises in the Old Testament (Deut. 10:17–18; 2 Sam. 7:14; Ps. 103:13) to the gospel proclamation in the New Testament (John 1:12; Rom. 8; Gal. 4; Eph. 1), the Father's heart is revealed in His adopting love. The Spirit testifies to this reality within us, confirming that we belong to Him, while Christ secures this adoption through His death and resurrection. Our identity, therefore, is not fragile or temporary but anchored in God's eternal declaration: *"You are my beloved child."*

Themes

The doctrine of the imago Dei introduces us to our identity as image-bearers of God, but the gospel takes us far deeper into the mystery of grace. Creation bestowed dignity; redemption bestows adoption. In Christ, we are not merely God's handiwork but His household. We are not merely fashioned from dust and spirit but welcomed into the embrace of divine family. Scripture never leaves us with the cold identity of servants alone, nor reduces us to subjects of a distant monarch. Rather, it proclaims something staggering: we are sons and daughters of the Most High, called by His name, sealed with His Spirit, and promised His kingdom.

This adoption is supernatural, not natural. It is not traced through genealogy, bloodline, or ethnic claim. It does not belong to the will of flesh, nor to the striving of humanity (John 1:12–13). It is the Spirit of God who awakens faith, who calls the dead to life, who brings near those once far away (Eph. 2:13). To be called a son or daughter of God is to be grafted into a family we did not deserve, to be clothed with a robe we did not earn, and to sit at a table where once we had no seat. Adoption is the gracious act of God through which strangers become children, rebels become heirs, and sinners become beloved.

This new identity transforms every dimension of our existence. It confers privileges, cultivates intimacy, and carries responsibilities. To name God as Father is to receive a new name, a new heritage, and a new destiny. We no longer live as orphans scrambling for approval or as slaves trembling in fear, but as children who know the Father's voice, trust His heart, and anticipate His inheritance.

Inheritance

Paul's words in Romans 8:17 are breathtaking: "If children, then heirs—heirs of God and fellow heirs with Christ." With one phrase, the apostle moves us from the

language of relationship to the language of inheritance.
Adoption in Christ is not sentimental—it is covenantal.
It grants legal standing in the divine household, full
rights to promises that can never be revoked. To be
God's child is to be named in His will, to be guaranteed
a share in His kingdom, to be promised treasures that
moth and rust cannot destroy (Matt. 6:19–20).

What is this inheritance? Scripture paints it in
dazzling colors:

- **Eternal life:** "This is the promise that He made
  to us—eternal life." (1 John 2:25)

- **The resurrection of the body:** "He who raised
  the Lord Jesus will raise us also with Jesus and
  bring us with you into his presence." (2 Cor. 4:14;
  cf. 1 Cor. 15:52–53)

- **The indwelling Spirit:** "Who has also put His
  seal on us and given us His Spirit in our hearts as a
  guarantee." (2 Cor. 1:22)

- **The kingdom itself:** "Fear not, little flock, for it
  is your Father's good pleasure to give you the
  kingdom." (Luke 12:32)

- **The new heavens and new earth:** "According
  to his promise we are waiting for new heavens and
  a new earth in which righteousness dwells." (2 Pet.
  3:13)

- **God Himself:** "The LORD is my chosen portion
  and my cup; you hold my lot." (Ps. 16:5; cf. Lam.
  3:24)

Unlike earthly inheritances, this one "can never perish, spoil, or fade. This inheritance is kept in heaven for you" (1 Pet. 1:4). It is not subject to market crashes, legal disputes, or family quarrels. It is guaranteed by the unchanging will of the Father and sealed by the Spirit, who is both the down payment and the pledge of what is to come (Eph. 1:13–14). The Spirit whispers to our spirit that we belong to God, and in so doing, He assures us that the inheritance is certain.

How does this inheritance shape our present lives? It loosens our grip on what is passing away. We no longer cling desperately to earthly possessions, nor measure success by temporary gains. Jesus told His followers not to store up treasures on earth but in heaven (Matt. 6:19–21), and Paul echoed this by calling us to "set your minds on things above, not on earthly things" (Col. 3:2). To know that you are an heir of God is to live with freedom from anxiety, envy, and greed. If all the riches of the Father's house are yours in Christ, why envy the world's trinkets?

This inheritance also reframes suffering. Paul ties the two realities together: "if indeed we suffer with Him, that we may also be glorified with Him" (Rom. 8:17). Present trials are no longer meaningless or random—they are labor pains of glory, preparation for the inheritance. As he writes elsewhere, "this light momentary affliction is preparing for us an eternal weight of glory beyond all comparison" (2 Cor. 4:17). Every tear will be wiped away (Rev. 21:4), every injustice will be answered, every sacrifice for Christ will be rewarded. To live as heirs is to endure hardship with the steady confidence that glory awaits.

The Old Testament anticipation. The theme of inheritance runs throughout Scripture. Israel inherited the promised land (Deut. 26:1), not as a reward for merit but as a gift from their covenant Father. The land was a foretaste of a greater inheritance still to come. The Levites, uniquely, were told, "The LORD is your inheritance" (Num. 18:20), foreshadowing the ultimate reality that God Himself is the true portion of His children. In Christ, all believers receive what the Levites tasted: God as their inheritance, presence as their treasure, communion as their reward.

The New Testament fulfillment. In Christ, the shadows become substance. Peter describes believers as "a chosen race, a royal priesthood" (1 Pet. 2:9), echoing Israel's calling but extending it universally to the church. Paul assures us in Galatians 3:29: "If you belong to Christ, then you are Abraham's seed, and heirs according to the promise." The promises given to Abraham—blessing, offspring, inheritance—are fulfilled in Christ and shared with all who are united to Him by faith. Thus, Jew and Gentile together are "fellow heirs, members of the same body, and partakers of the promise in Christ Jesus through the gospel" (Eph. 3:6).

Practical implications:

1. **Generosity:** Knowing we have a secure inheritance frees us to give generously now. We

can live open-handed because our treasure is guaranteed in heaven (Matt. 6:20).

2. **Holiness:** Children who will inherit their Father's kingdom must reflect His character. "Everyone who thus hopes in him purifies himself as he is pure" (1 John 3:3).

3. **Hope in death:** Inheritance gives Christians unique confidence in the face of mortality. As Paul said, "to live is Christ, and to die is gain" (Phil. 1:21).

4. **Perseverance:** When suffering presses hard, inheritance reminds us of what lies beyond. "Be faithful unto death, and I will give you the crown of life" (Rev. 2:10).

5. **Unity:** Since the inheritance is shared, rivalry has no place. The same Father has promised the same eternal kingdom to all His children.

A devotional vision: Imagine the Father handing you a sealed document with your name written in His own hand. It declares that everything that belongs to His Son belongs also to you: resurrection, glory, eternal joy. The Spirit within you whispers, "Yes, it is true. You are His heir." That document cannot be forged, revoked, or misplaced. It is sealed with the blood of Christ and secured by the faithfulness of God Himself. This is not merely a promise of the future—it is power for the present. It calls you to walk with confidence, endure with hope, and live with joy.

To live as heirs is to recognize that the crown is already promised, the treasure already secured, the kingdom already ours. Our inheritance is not just life everlasting, but life with God Himself—the ultimate gift and the final goal of adoption.

Intimacy

Adoption is not merely a legal transaction but a relational miracle. It does not stop at new status; it ushers us into new closeness. Galatians 4:6 declares: "Because you are sons, God sent the Spirit of his Son into our hearts, the Spirit who calls out, 'Abba, Father.'" That small word—"Abba"—is a term of intimacy, affection, and trust, a word children used for their fathers. It signals not cold formality but warm nearness. Through Christ, God is no longer distant, unreachable, or hidden. He is our Father, and we are His children.

Biblical witness to intimacy with God:

- **Jesus' own prayers:** In Gethsemane, Jesus cried, "Abba, Father, all things are possible for you" (Mark 14:36). Through adoption, the same Spirit that was in Jesus teaches us to pray with that same intimacy.

- **Old Testament anticipation:** "As a father shows compassion to his children, so the LORD shows compassion to those who fear him" (Ps. 103:13). Israel knew God as Father corporately; believers in Christ know Him personally.

- **Assurance in prayer:** "In him and through faith in him we may approach God with freedom and confidence" (Eph. 3:12). Adoption gives us boldness to come before the throne without fear.

- **Jesus' teaching:** "Your Father knows what you need before you ask him" (Matt. 6:8). Intimacy is rooted in trust that our Father sees, cares, and provides.

How intimacy changes prayer and worship: Prayer is no longer a desperate attempt to persuade a reluctant deity but the natural conversation of a child with a Father who delights to hear. Worship is no longer mere duty but the overflow of love and gratitude. Daily life is infused with the Father's presence—when rising, working, eating, or resting, we are never alone, for His Spirit abides within (John 14:23).

This intimacy heals deep wounds. Many live under the shadow of rejection, fear, or shame, but adoption tells a different story: "The Spirit you received does not make you slaves, so that you live in fear again; rather, the Spirit you received brought about your adoption" (Rom. 8:15). Fear whispers, "You are unwanted." Shame says, "You are unworthy." Adoption silences both with the Father's voice: "You are mine. You are beloved. You are my child."

Practical implications of intimacy:

1. **Confidence in prayer:** Hebrews 4:16 commands us to "approach God's throne of grace with

confidence." Adoption guarantees our welcome.

2. **Freedom from fear:** Perfect love drives out fear (1 John 4:18). The Father's love replaces anxiety with peace.

3. **Daily assurance:** Even in failure, the Spirit testifies to our belonging (Rom. 8:16).

4. **Joy in obedience:** Children obey not to earn love but because they are loved. "If you love me, keep my commandments" (John 14:15).

To live in intimacy is to walk in constant awareness of God's fatherly presence. He is not a far-off monarch but a near and tender Father. This reality is the heartbeat of Christian life, the fountain from which prayer, worship, and joy overflow. Adoption brings us home—not just legally, but relationally.

Responsibility

Adoption carries with it privilege, but also responsibility. If we are God's children, we must reflect His character. Just as earthly children resemble their parents in mannerisms or appearance, so spiritual children must take on the likeness of their Father. Paul makes this explicit: "Therefore be imitators of God, as beloved children. And walk in love, as Christ loved us and gave himself up for us" (Eph. 5:1–2).

Scriptural foundation for responsibility:

- **Holiness:** "Be holy, because I am holy" (Lev. 11:44; echoed in 1 Pet. 1:16). Adoption into God's family calls for family resemblance in holiness.

- **Love:** "Love your enemies and pray for those who persecute you, that you may be children of your Father in heaven" (Matt. 5:44–45).

- **Mercy:** "Be merciful, even as your Father is merciful" (Luke 6:36).

- **Truth:** Children of the Father walk in truth, for "it is impossible for God to lie" (Heb. 6:18).

- **Purity:** "Everyone who has this hope in him purifies himself, just as he is pure" (1 John 3:3).

Family resemblance in action: To carry the name of the Father is to bear witness to His reputation. The world looks at the children to know something about the parent. Jesus warns in John 8:44 that those who lie and hate show themselves children of the devil, while those who love and obey mark themselves as children of God. The contrast is stark: adoption is revealed by resemblance.

Responsibility in the church and world: If God is our Father, then fellow believers are brothers and sisters. Responsibility means practicing forgiveness (Col. 3:13), serving one another (Gal. 5:13), and pursuing unity (Eph. 4:3). Outside the church, it means representing the Father's kingdom in word and deed, shining as "children of God without fault in a warped and crooked generation" (Phil. 2:15).

Practical implications of responsibility:

1. **Moral conduct:** As heirs of holiness, we are called to resist sin and walk in righteousness (Rom. 6:12–14).

2. **Generosity:** As children of a generous Father, we give freely (2 Cor. 9:7).

3. **Peacemaking:** "Blessed are the peacemakers, for they will be called children of God" (Matt. 5:9).

4. **Witness:** Our words and actions tell the world who our Father is (Matt. 5:16).

5. **Endurance:** Discipline is not rejection but proof of sonship (Heb. 12:6–7).

The weight and joy of responsibility: Responsibility is not drudgery but delight. Just as children often want to "be like Dad" or "be like Mom," believers long to reflect their Father's heart. Obedience is the fruit of belonging, not the condition of it. "For this is the love of God, that we keep his commandments. And his commandments are not burdensome" (1 John 5:3).

Thus, responsibility means living with reverence, gratitude, and faithfulness. It means carrying the Father's name with honor, guarding the unity of the household, and displaying the family likeness of holiness, mercy, and love. To be God's child is to live as a living picture of the Father in the world.

Adoption and the Church

Being sons and daughters changes not only how we relate to God but how we relate to one another. If God is our Father, then fellow believers are not acquaintances or strangers but brothers and sisters bound in a covenant family. The apostle Paul declares, "You are no longer strangers and aliens, but you are fellow citizens with the saints and members of the household of God" (Eph. 2:19). The church is not a social club, a voluntary association, or a loose collection of like-minded individuals—it is God's household, built on the foundation of Christ Himself (Eph. 2:20–22). Its bonds are stronger than culture, class, race, or personal preference, because its glue is the blood of Jesus Christ shed for our adoption.

Unity as covenantal, not optional. Unity in the church flows directly from our adoption. If God has received us as sons and daughters, then we must receive one another as brothers and sisters. Paul exhorts, "Accept one another, then, just as Christ accepted you, in order to bring praise to God" (Rom. 15:7). Division, prejudice, and rivalry are not minor infractions but betrayals of the family identity. To despise a brother or sister is to despise one for whom Christ died (Rom. 14:15). To love them, despite differences and struggles, is to honor the Father whose household we share.

Forgiveness as covenantal, not sentimental. This new family identity reframes forgiveness. Within the household of God, grudges are contradictions, and bitterness becomes rebellion against the Father's love. Jesus taught His disciples to pray daily, "Forgive us our debts, as we also have forgiven our debtors" (Matt. 6:12). Forgiveness is not optional or peripheral; it is essential to family life. We forgive not merely because it feels right but because the Father has forgiven us an infinite debt (Matt. 18:21–35). A reconciled family must practice reconciliation. Failure to forgive is not simply a private grievance but an act of disloyalty to the Father's household.

Love as the family resemblance. Jesus told His disciples, "By this all people will know that you are my disciples, if you love one another" (John 13:35). Love is the family resemblance of God's children. Just as children often bear their parents' features, so too the sons and daughters of God are to be marked by sacrificial, patient, enduring love. Paul describes this in 1 Corinthians 13: love that is patient and kind, not arrogant or rude, rejoicing with the truth, enduring all things. Such love is not natural but supernatural, produced by the Spirit within the adopted children of God.

The church as a new household. Adoption also redefines what "family" means. Jesus Himself said, "Whoever does the will of my Father in heaven is my brother and sister and mother" (Matt. 12:50). The bonds of the gospel family sometimes surpass even biological ties. This does not diminish the natural family but situates it within a larger household of faith. In the church, widows find children, orphans find parents, strangers find kin. "God sets the lonely in families" (Ps. 68:6), and the church becomes the living fulfillment of that promise.

Implications for daily life:

1. **Hospitality:** To treat fellow believers as family means welcoming them into our homes and hearts (Rom. 12:13; Heb. 13:2).

2. **Mutual care:** When one suffers, all suffer; when one rejoices, all rejoice (1 Cor. 12:26).

3. **Equality:** In Christ there is neither Jew nor Greek, slave nor free, male nor female—we are all one (Gal. 3:28).

4. **Accountability:** Brothers and sisters exhort and correct one another in love (Gal. 6:1–2; Heb. 3:13).

5. **Worship:** Gathered worship is not an event but a family meal around the Father's table (1 Cor. 10:16–17).

Thus, adoption makes the church not a voluntary society but a supernatural family, bound by covenant love and united by the Spirit of the Son. It is in the church that the reality of our adoption is displayed most vividly: reconciled sinners living as one household under one Father.

Adoption and Mission

Finally, adoption shapes not only our family life within the church but also our witness to the world. In a culture marked by loneliness, fragmentation, and spiritual orphanhood, the church's testimony must be to embody the Father's welcome. The gospel does not only declare forgiveness of sins; it proclaims the astonishing truth that God makes enemies into children and strangers into heirs. Evangelism is therefore not merely convincing arguments or winning debates—it is extending the Father's invitation into His family.

The Father's heart revealed. John exclaims, "See what great love the Father has lavished on us, that we should be called children of God! And that is what we are!" (1 John 3:1). Adoption is itself a message to the world. Our testimony is not only that God saves but that He adopts, that He seats the poor and the broken at His table, clothing them with robes of righteousness and giving them a name and an inheritance. This is why the early church was so magnetic—its fellowship embodied the love of a Father who gathers prodigals home (Luke 15:20–24).

Mission as family extension. When we share the gospel, we are not merely offering ideas; we are extending a welcome. Paul describes his ministry in family terms: "We were gentle among you, like a nursing mother taking care of her own children" (1 Thess. 2:7), and again, "We exhorted each one of you and encouraged you and charged you to walk in a manner worthy of God, who calls you into his own kingdom and glory" (1 Thess. 2:12). Mission is adoption-shaped: a family inviting others to the Father's household.

Countercultural witness. In a fragmented world defined by isolation, racial hostility, and economic inequality, adoption provides a radical counter-testimony. When the church embodies unity across divisions, it demonstrates that God truly is creating one new family out of many peoples (Eph. 2:14–16). Evangelism gains credibility when outsiders see not only doctrine but fellowship, not only words but welcome. Jesus prayed that His disciples "may be one... so that the world may believe that you have sent me" (John 17:21). Unity and adoption are missionary tools.

Practical outworking of adoption in mission:

1. **Hospitality to strangers:** Welcoming the outsider models the Father's heart (Rom. 15:7).

2. **Care for orphans and widows:** "Religion that God our Father accepts as pure and faultless is this: to look after orphans and widows" (James 1:27). Adoption compels us to reflect God's concern for the vulnerable.

3. **Evangelism as invitation:** The gospel message is: "Come home. The Father is waiting."

4. **Cross-cultural mission:** Adoption unites Jew and Gentile, slave and free, rich and poor (Eph. 3:6). This compels mission across barriers.

5. **Mercy ministries:** Feeding the hungry, sheltering the homeless, visiting the prisoner are all family acts of extending the Father's love (Matt. 25:35–36).

A prophetic witness. In a world that often leaves people spiritually orphaned—adrift without identity, security, or belonging—the church proclaims a better word: you are invited into the family of God. The story of the prodigal son (Luke 15) becomes a living parable: the Father runs to embrace the lost, clothing them with honor, restoring their place at the table. Every act of evangelism and service becomes a reenactment of this welcome.

Summary. Adoption into God's family grants us **inheritance** that secures our future, **intimacy** that redefines our present, and **responsibility** that directs our conduct. It transforms our vertical relationship with God and our horizontal relationships with others. It grounds our worship, sustains our hope, demands our holiness, and fuels our mission. To live as sons and daughters of the Most High is to embrace both privilege and responsibility, both nearness and accountability, both present grace and future glory. The church becomes the family of God, and mission becomes the family invitation—"Come home to the Father, for you too can be His child."

Reflection

As you consider the doctrine of adoption and your identity as a son or daughter of the Most High, take time to pause, examine, and pray through the following extended reflections. Let these questions and prompts stretch across different areas of life—your heart, relationships, worship, suffering, and mission.

- **Identity and Assurance:** Do you live as though you are God's beloved child, or do you often slip back into fear, shame, or striving as though you were still a slave (Rom. 8:15)? What changes in your daily outlook if you truly rest in your Father's love each morning? How might assurance in His adoption quiet the restless search for approval from others?

- **Inheritance and Hope:** What does "inheritance with Christ" (Rom. 8:17) mean for your daily life? Does it change how you see success, wealth, and ambition? How does it reframe your view of suffering, knowing that "our present sufferings are not worth comparing with the glory that will be revealed in us" (Rom. 8:18)? Where do you need to remind yourself that trials are birth pangs of glory?

- **Relationships and Community:** How might your friendships, family life, and work relationships change if you truly saw others as God's sons and daughters—your brothers and sisters in Christ? What would shift in the way you speak, forgive, serve, and encourage them (Eph. 4:32)? Could you name one relationship that needs to be reoriented around this truth?

- **Prayer and Intimacy:** In your prayers, do you approach God as "Abba, Father" (Gal. 4:6), or do you slip into distant formality, as if He were uninterested or far away? How can you cultivate childlike trust in His presence—perhaps by praying the Lord's Prayer slowly, journaling prayers, or simply sitting silently in His love? What difference would intimacy make in how you handle anxiety or fear (Phil. 4:6–7)?

- **Spiritual Practices:** Which practices—Scripture meditation, journaling, confession, fasting, corporate worship, Sabbath rest—remind you most powerfully of your identity as a child of God? Which of these rhythms might the Spirit be inviting you to strengthen this week? How might these practices shift from duty to delight when seen through the lens of family life with your Father?

- **Struggles to Believe:** Where do you find it hardest to believe that God has truly adopted you? Is it in moments of guilt over past sin, fear of rejection, or feelings of unworthiness? Bring these doubts honestly before your Father in prayer (Ps. 34:18). What promises of Scripture can you cling to in these moments (e.g., John 10:28–29; Heb. 13:5)?

- **Guarding Against Pride and Despair:** How does adoption protect you from both pride and despair? Pride has no place because this identity is received by grace, not earned (Eph. 2:8–9).

Despair has no place because the Father never abandons His children (Deut. 31:6). Where are you tempted to boast, and where are you tempted to despair? How does adoption answer both?

- **Witness and Daily Life:** What would it look like to embody this identity at work, in your family, or in your neighborhood? Could others see in your life the peace, joy, and security that flow from belonging to God? How might your adoption shape the way you respond to criticism, deal with conflict, or serve those in need?

- **The Church as Family:** How does adoption into God's household (Eph. 2:19) shape your view of the church? Do you treat fellow believers as true spiritual siblings, or more as casual acquaintances? How might this truth change the way you participate in worship, hospitality, and service? What specific act of family love could you extend to someone in your congregation this week?

- **Privilege and Responsibility:** How do you hold together both the privilege and the responsibility of being God's child? Privilege gives you access, intimacy, and inheritance; responsibility calls you to holiness, mercy, and mission. Which side do you tend to neglect—resting in privilege without obedience, or laboring in responsibility without resting in grace? What rhythms might help you balance both?

- **Discipline as Love:** Hebrews 12:6 reminds us that "the Lord disciplines the one he loves." How do you respond to the Father's discipline in your life? Do you see it as rejection or as proof of sonship? How might viewing trials as loving correction reshape your endurance and gratitude?

- **Future Glory:** How does the promise of future inheritance—resurrection, new creation, eternal fellowship with the Father—encourage you in seasons of suffering? Do you allow the hope of glory (Col. 1:27) to fuel endurance today? How might you keep this hope more visible, perhaps through journaling promises, memorizing key Scriptures, or sharing testimonies of hope with others?

- **Forgiveness and Reconciliation:** Adoption into one family means forgiving one another as God forgave us (Col. 3:13). Is there someone you need to forgive or be reconciled with in the family of God? What practical step could you take to embody covenantal forgiveness, not just personal sentiment?

- **Mission as Invitation:** How does knowing your adoption influence the way you share the gospel? Do you see evangelism less as argument and more as invitation—"Come home to the Father"? Who in your life might be waiting for such an invitation today?

Take time with these questions slowly—perhaps one per day in prayer and journaling. Let the Spirit search your heart, remind you of the Father's love, and call you into deeper trust, obedience, and joy.

Chapter 3

The Kingdom Within

Scripture Foundation

"The kingdom of God does not come with observation; nor will they say, 'See here!' or 'See there!' For indeed, the kingdom of God is within you." (Luke 17:20–21)

Exegesis of Luke 17:20–21

The context of Jesus' statement is His dialogue with the Pharisees, who asked when the kingdom of God would come (Luke 17:20). Their question reveals the common expectation of the time: that the kingdom would be a visible, political, and national restoration of Israel. Many longed for a Messiah who would overthrow Roman occupation, restore the throne of David, and inaugurate a reign marked by military victory and outward display. The Pharisees, steeped in meticulous observation of the Law and eager for external signs, expected the kingdom to be discernible by dramatic, observable events.

Jesus overturns those assumptions. He responds, "The kingdom of God does not come with observation." The word for "observation" (*paratērēsis*) carries the sense of close scrutiny, watching for visible signs, as one might scan the sky for omens. Jesus is clear: God's reign cannot be tracked with calculations or observed with political eyes. It does not arrive through census or spectacle, thrones or armies. Instead, He insists, the kingdom is already present, already active, already breaking into human life through His own ministry.

The Greek phrase: "within you" or "in your midst." At the heart of Jesus' saying lies the phrase *entos hymōn*. Translators have long debated its meaning. It can be rendered:

- **"Within you"** — emphasizing internal transformation, the reign of God taking root in the heart through repentance, faith, and the Spirit's indwelling. This interpretation highlights the personal, spiritual reality of God's kingdom, not merely external institutions.

- **"In your midst"** — emphasizing the presence of the King Himself among them. The kingdom is not hidden within the Pharisees' hearts (since many resisted Jesus), but embodied in Christ, who was physically standing in their midst as the living manifestation of God's rule.

Both carry weight, and together they provide a fuller picture. The kingdom begins in Christ—the King present in their midst—and extends through His people as it takes root within hearts. Christ Himself is the kingdom embodied; His followers become the kingdom manifested as they live under His reign.

Historical and theological context. First-century Jews were saturated with kingdom expectation. The Psalms celebrated God's reign over the nations (Ps. 93:1; 97:1). The prophets foresaw a day when God would restore His people and reign visibly from Zion (Isa. 2:2–4; Mic. 4:1–3). Apocalyptic literature, such as the visions in Daniel 7, promised that "the saints of the Most High shall receive the kingdom and possess it forever" (Dan. 7:18). The Pharisees asked Jesus about timing because they were looking for a visible, cataclysmic arrival. Jesus reframes their entire paradigm: the kingdom is not primarily about external overthrow but about inward renewal and divine presence.

The convergence of meanings. Both translations—"within you" and "in your midst"—find fulfillment in the gospel:

1. **The Kingdom "in your midst":** Jesus Himself is the King. Wherever He goes, the kingdom goes. His miracles are signs of the kingdom's power breaking into the present age (Luke 11:20). His teaching reveals the kingdom's values. His presence inaugurates God's reign in history.

2. **The Kingdom "within you":** Through the

Spirit, the kingdom takes residence in the believer's heart. Ezekiel's promise of a new heart and new spirit (Ezek. 36:26–27) is fulfilled in those who follow Christ. Paul later echoes this when he declares, "The kingdom of God is not a matter of eating and drinking, but of righteousness, peace, and joy in the Holy Spirit" (Rom. 14:17).

Thus, Jesus' words are not contradictory but complementary: the King was among them, and His reign would be established within all who believe.

Parallels and echoes in Scripture. Jesus' teaching here resonates with other passages:

- In John 18:36, Jesus tells Pilate, "My kingdom is not of this world," rejecting the idea of a political revolt and pointing instead to a spiritual reign.

- In Matthew 12:28, He declares, "If I drive out demons by the Spirit of God, then the kingdom of God has come upon you." The kingdom is present where the King exercises authority.

- In Colossians 1:13, Paul writes, "He has delivered us from the domain of darkness and transferred us to the kingdom of his beloved Son." This transfer is spiritual and present, not merely future.

Each passage confirms that the kingdom is not postponed to a distant age but inaugurated in Christ's coming, revealed in His ministry, and advanced in the Spirit's work.

Implications of Jesus' statement. By saying the kingdom is already among them, Jesus exposed the blindness of the Pharisees. They searched the skies for cosmic signs yet failed to recognize the King standing in front of them. This is a sobering warning: the kingdom may be nearer than we think, but it is missed if our eyes are set on the wrong expectations.

Moreover, His words call disciples to inward examination. The question is not merely, "Where is the kingdom coming?" but "Who reigns in your heart?" God's kingdom is not limited to geography or institutions; it is revealed wherever His will is obeyed, His Spirit dwells, and His presence is honored.

Summary. The exegesis of Luke 17:20–21 shows that Jesus radically redefined kingdom expectation. Against the Pharisees' obsession with signs, He declared the kingdom to be both present and hidden, both inward and embodied. The Greek phrase *entos hymōn* holds together the truth that Christ is the kingdom in their midst and that His Spirit establishes the kingdom within His followers. Thus, the kingdom is not primarily an external spectacle but the reign of God manifest in Christ, implanted in hearts, and growing outward until it fills the earth.

The Broader Biblical Witness

The idea of God's kingdom as an inward and spiritual reality is not limited to one verse in Luke 17. It flows like a golden thread through the entire biblical narrative,

from the promises of the prophets to the teaching of
Jesus, the letters of Paul, and the hope of Revelation.
Scripture testifies consistently that God's reign is not
confined to thrones, borders, or armies—it begins in
hearts reborn by grace and expands outward into the
world.

The Prophets' Hope. Long before Christ's coming,
the prophets spoke of a day when God's rule would
penetrate not only the structures of nations but the very
hearts of His people. Ezekiel 36:26–27 declares: "I will
give you a new heart and put a new spirit in you; I will
remove from you your heart of stone and give you a
heart of flesh. And I will put my Spirit in you and move
you to follow my decrees." The kingdom here is inward,
spiritual, and transformative. Jeremiah echoes the same
hope: "This is the covenant I will make with the people
of Israel after that time... I will put my law in their
minds and write it on their hearts. I will be their God,
and they will be my people" (Jer. 31:33). The kingdom
does not come through external force but through
internal renewal by God's Spirit.

Isaiah envisioned a Servant whose reign would establish
justice not by shouting or crushing but by gentle
faithfulness: "A bruised reed he will not break, and a
smoldering wick he will not snuff out" (Isa. 42:3). The
prophets point to a reign that begins in transformation
and mercy, not military conquest.

The Kingdom in the Teaching of Jesus. Jesus'
parables consistently emphasize the hidden, growing,

inward reality of the kingdom. In Matthew 13, He compares the kingdom to:

- A mustard seed, the smallest of seeds, which grows into a tree where birds nest (Matt. 13:31–32). God's reign starts small but expands quietly until it blesses the nations.

- Yeast that a woman mixes into flour until it works through the whole batch (Matt. 13:33). The kingdom is invisible in its working yet unstoppable in its effect.

- A treasure hidden in a field and a pearl of great price (Matt. 13:44–46). The kingdom's value is discovered inwardly by those who recognize it, compelling them to surrender all else.

In Luke 8:11–15, the parable of the sower teaches that the kingdom's word must be received in the heart like seed in good soil. The kingdom is not enforced from the outside but welcomed within, where it bears fruit.

Jesus also taught that the kingdom is present in His ministry: "If I drive out demons by the Spirit of God, then the kingdom of God has come upon you" (Matt. 12:28). Wherever Christ reigns—in healing, in deliverance, in forgiveness—the kingdom is present. Yet it remains hidden to those without spiritual eyes: "The kingdom of God is like a man who scatters seed on the ground... night and day, whether he sleeps or gets up, the seed sprouts and grows, though he does not know how" (Mark 4:26–27). The kingdom is real, active, and growing, even when unnoticed.

The Kingdom and the Sermon on the Mount. In
Matthew 5–7, Jesus presents the ethics of the kingdom,
rooted not in outward conformity but in inward
transformation. "Blessed are the pure in heart, for they
shall see God" (Matt. 5:8). Anger, lust, pride, and
anxiety are addressed at the heart level. The Lord's
Prayer teaches disciples to pray, "Thy kingdom come,
thy will be done, on earth as it is in heaven" (Matt.
6:10). The kingdom advances as God's will is embraced
internally and enacted externally.

The Kingdom in Paul's Vision. Paul takes up the
theme with clarity: "The kingdom of God is not a
matter of eating and drinking, but of righteousness,
peace, and joy in the Holy Spirit" (Rom. 14:17). For
Paul, the kingdom is not ceremonial regulation but the
Spirit's work within believers. He teaches that believers
have already been "transferred into the kingdom of His
beloved Son" (Col. 1:13). This transfer is spiritual,
present, and real. The reign of God is experienced
wherever Christ is Lord and the Spirit empowers
obedience.

In 1 Corinthians 4:20, Paul insists: "The kingdom of
God is not a matter of talk but of power." This is not
political power but the power of the Spirit changing lives.
Galatians 5:22–23 describes the fruit of that inward
reign—love, joy, peace, patience, kindness, goodness,
faithfulness, gentleness, and self-control. These are not
imposed by law but produced by God's Spirit ruling
within.

Christ in Us. Paul captures the inwardness of the kingdom in Colossians 1:27: "Christ in you, the hope of glory." The kingdom is not primarily external structures but Christ dwelling in His people. Believers are temples of the Spirit (1 Cor. 6:19), and where the King dwells, His kingdom is manifest. The reign of God begins with Christ's presence in us, shaping our desires, guiding our choices, and empowering our witness.

The Kingdom and John's Writings. John records Jesus telling Nicodemus, "Unless one is born again he cannot see the kingdom of God" (John 3:3). The kingdom is invisible to the natural eye; it requires new birth to perceive and enter. Later, Jesus tells His disciples, "The kingdom is not of this world" (John 18:36), underlining again that His reign is not political or geographical but spiritual and eternal. The Apostle John later sees in Revelation the ultimate fulfillment: "The kingdom of the world has become the kingdom of our Lord and of his Christ, and he shall reign forever and ever" (Rev. 11:15). What begins inwardly in hearts will one day be revealed outwardly over all creation.

Consistent Testimony Across Scripture. From Moses to the prophets, from Jesus to Paul and John, the witness is consistent: God's rule begins not with armies, borders, or political decrees but with hearts made new by His Spirit. It is inward before it is outward, spiritual before it is visible. It is yeast working through dough, a seed sprouting in the soil, a treasure hidden until revealed. It is Christ present among His people and Christ present within them. The kingdom is both now and not yet—already present in the Spirit's work, yet awaiting its full unveiling when Christ returns.

Summary. The broader biblical witness confirms Jesus' claim: the kingdom is not found by scanning the skies or waiting for thrones. It is discovered in new hearts, in hidden growth, in righteousness, peace, and joy in the Holy Spirit. It is the reign of Christ in our midst and within us. And though the world still waits for the day when the kingdom is fully revealed, those who belong to Christ already taste its power, live in its reality, and carry its presence wherever they go.

What Jesus Wants Us to Realize

Jesus calls His hearers to a profound shift of vision, a redefinition of the kingdom that cuts across human assumptions. The Pharisees looked for signs in the sky—astrological portents, cosmic upheavals, or political events that would herald God's reign. Jesus pointed instead to the Spirit's quiet work in the soul. The people hoped for Rome's overthrow, longing for a Davidic king who would restore Israel's national pride. Jesus announced the overthrow of something deeper: the tyranny of sin, the power of Satan, and the sting of death itself. The crowds expected a throne in Jerusalem, complete with legions and banners. Jesus offered a cross outside Jerusalem, a resurrection in a garden, and a Spirit poured out at Pentecost that would plant God's kingdom in every land.

Not merely future, but already present. The
central point of Jesus' teaching is that the kingdom of
God is not only future—something to be waited for when
Christ returns in glory—but also present, unfolding here
and now. When He taught His disciples to pray, "Thy
kingdom come, Thy will be done, on earth as it is in
heaven" (Matt. 6:10), He revealed that the kingdom is
experienced wherever God's will is embraced and
enacted. The reign of God is not distant, abstract, or
inaccessible; it is as near as the repentant heart, as real
as faith, as tangible as love expressed in action. Every
act of forgiveness, every work of mercy, every moment of
surrender to God's will is a present manifestation of the
kingdom.

The hidden but unstoppable reign. Jesus often
described the kingdom in parables that emphasize its
hidden yet unstoppable nature. The mustard seed begins
almost imperceptibly small but grows into a tree that
shelters the nations (Matt. 13:31–32). The yeast works
invisibly in the dough until the whole batch is leavened
(Matt. 13:33). The kingdom does not arrive with fanfare
or armies but with quiet, transformative power. To
realize this is to understand that God's reign is not
fragile, not contingent on human politics, but inexorable
and certain, spreading through the world and through
history until it fills the earth (Hab. 2:14).

The inward conquest. What Jesus wants us to see is
that the greatest enemy is not Rome but the human
heart enslaved to sin. The kingdom is not first about the
liberation of nations but about the liberation of souls.

"Everyone who sins is a slave to sin... but if the Son sets you free, you will be free indeed" (John 8:34–36). The real revolution takes place not in palaces or senates but in consciences made clean, minds renewed, and spirits reborn. When a sinner repents, the kingdom has broken in. When a heart bows before Christ, the reign of God is established.

The presence of the King. To realize the kingdom is to recognize the King. Jesus says, "The kingdom of God is in your midst" (Luke 17:21), because He Himself is the embodiment of God's reign. Where Christ is present, the kingdom is present. His miracles were not mere displays of power but signs of the kingdom breaking into the present age: demons cast out (Luke 11:20), the sick healed, the poor lifted, sins forgiven. In His person, the reign of God is inaugurated. To miss Him is to miss the kingdom; to receive Him is to receive the kingdom.

The cross and resurrection as enthronement. Jesus wants us to realize that the kingdom does not come through conquest but through sacrifice. His throne is the cross; His coronation is the resurrection. In the eyes of the world, the cross was defeat. In the eyes of heaven, it was victory over sin and death. The resurrection was not merely proof of His divinity but the beginning of new creation, the dawn of the kingdom's fullness. When Jesus rose, the future age broke into the present, and the kingdom began to spread across the earth through His Spirit-filled church.

The Spirit as kingdom power. At Pentecost, the

Spirit came as wind and fire (Acts 2:1–4), empowering
the disciples to bear witness "to the ends of the earth"
(Acts 1:8). What Jesus wants us to grasp is that the
kingdom is not advanced by swords or coercion but by
the Spirit's transforming work. The Spirit convicts of sin,
opens blind eyes, grants new birth, and empowers
witness. The kingdom grows not through force but
through faith, not through armies but through
ambassadors of reconciliation (2 Cor. 5:20).

The kingdom now and not yet. Jesus balances two
truths: the kingdom is already here, and yet it is not yet
fully revealed. Already, Christ reigns in hearts and
communities where His Spirit dwells. Already, His
authority is proclaimed over sin, death, and the devil.
Yet the final consummation awaits His return, when He
will make all things new (Rev. 21:5). This tension—the
"already and not yet"—is central to the New Testament.
To realize the kingdom is to live in this tension,
experiencing its present power while longing for its final
unveiling.

Practical implications. To grasp what Jesus is saying
is to see life differently:

- It changes how we view suffering: trials are not
  signs of defeat but occasions for the kingdom's
  power to be revealed (2 Cor. 4:17).

- It changes how we view mission: evangelism is not
  mere persuasion but the extension of the kingdom's
  reign through proclamation and Spirit-power
  (Matt. 28:18–20).

- It changes how we view holiness: obedience is not legalism but the natural fruit of living under the King's reign (John 14:15).

- It changes how we view the church: the community of believers is an outpost of the kingdom, displaying God's rule to the world (Eph. 2:19–22).

Summary. What Jesus wants us to realize is that the kingdom is nearer than we think and greater than we imagine. It is not only future but present, not only external but internal, not only cosmic but personal. It is as near as your next prayer, as real as the Spirit's conviction, as powerful as love in action, as enduring as Christ's victory over the grave. The kingdom is already here, growing quietly yet inexorably, until the day when the King returns and the kingdom comes in full.

The Kingdom Within and the Kingdom Among

We must hold together both aspects of Jesus' words in Luke 17:21. The kingdom is not an either/or—either internal or external—but a both/and reality that is deeply personal and gloriously communal, invisible in its root yet visible in its fruit, present within believers yet revealed in the gathered body of Christ.

The Kingdom Within. The phrase "within you" points to the inner transformation that occurs when the Spirit indwells the believer. Paul writes, "Do you not

know that your body is a temple of the Holy Spirit
within you, whom you have from God?" (1 Cor. 6:19).
The believer's heart becomes the throne room of God,
the place where His will is done and His reign is
acknowledged. This inward kingdom is the fulfillment of
Ezekiel's prophecy: "I will put my Spirit within you, and
cause you to walk in my statutes" (Ezek. 36:27). The
reign of God begins not in palaces or parliaments but in
the human soul, reshaping desires, renewing minds, and
redirecting lives toward holiness.

This inner reign is also deeply practical. The kingdom
within you is seen in the fruit of the Spirit—love, joy,
peace, patience, kindness, goodness, faithfulness,
gentleness, self-control (Gal. 5:22–23). These are not
mere virtues but evidence of God's government taking
hold of a life. Every time a believer resists sin, forgives
an enemy, or serves with humility, the kingdom is
manifest within.

The Kingdom Among. Yet Jesus' words also carry
the sense of "in your midst." The kingdom was not only
hidden in hearts but standing bodily before them in the
person of Christ. He is the King in their midst,
embodying the reign of God through His words, miracles,
and authority. His exorcisms demonstrated the invasion
of God's power over Satan's dominion: "If it is by the
finger of God that I cast out demons, then the kingdom
of God has come upon you" (Luke 11:20). His healings
revealed God's compassion. His teachings unveiled God's
wisdom. To see Jesus was to see the kingdom in action.

Today, Christ's body—the church—continues to make

the kingdom visible in the world. Paul calls the church "God's household" (Eph. 2:19) and "a holy temple in the Lord" (Eph. 2:21). Wherever the church proclaims the gospel, practices forgiveness, shares bread, and cares for the least of these, the kingdom is made manifest among the nations. The kingdom among us is a communal reality: believers together form an embassy of heaven on earth.

Holding the Tension Together. If we emphasize only the kingdom within, we risk reducing it to private spirituality, detached from justice, community, and mission. If we emphasize only the kingdom among, we risk focusing on external structures without inward transformation. Jesus insists we hold both: the kingdom begins in the heart but does not stay there; it flows outward into relationships, communities, and societies. It is both deeply personal and inherently public. It is invisible in its seed but visible in its harvest.

Practical Implications.

1. **For the Individual:** Are you allowing the Spirit to reign in your thoughts, words, and desires? The kingdom within is evidenced by daily surrender and growth in holiness.

2. **For the Church:** Do our congregations reflect the kingdom among us through love, unity, and mission? The watching world should see in the church a foretaste of God's reign.

3. **For Society:** The kingdom's presence calls us to

justice, mercy, and compassion in public life (Mic. 6:8). It challenges exploitation and embodies peace.

4. **For Mission:** We proclaim not only an inner transformation but also a visible fellowship into which others are invited. The kingdom spreads as hearts are changed and as communities embody Christ's love.

Summary. The kingdom within you makes the believer a temple of the Spirit; the kingdom among you makes the church a temple in the world. Together, these truths prevent us from narrowing God's reign to either private piety or public activism. The kingdom is both—personal and communal, inward and outward, spiritual and visible. It begins in the heart but overflows into justice, mercy, and mission until the knowledge of the Lord covers the earth as the waters cover the sea (Hab. 2:14).

Practical Implications

The teaching that the kingdom of God is both within and among us is not abstract theology but a reality that reshapes every dimension of life. Jesus' words press us to examine how God's reign transforms our hearts, directs our daily obedience, defines our community life, and propels our mission. To live as kingdom people is to live differently in thought, word, and deed.

1. **Personal Transformation:** The kingdom begins in you. Jesus insists that true transformation is not external ritual but inward renewal. "Unless one is

born again, he cannot see the kingdom of God"
(John 3:3). This means that entry into the kingdom
is spiritual rebirth, a miracle of grace where the
Spirit gives new life, new desires, and new
affections. Are you allowing the Spirit to reign in
your thoughts, desires, and actions? Paul exhorts
us to "be transformed by the renewal of your mind"
(Rom. 12:2), for the kingdom reshapes not only
what we do but how we think, feel, and perceive.
Personal transformation is seen in the fruit of the
Spirit (Gal. 5:22–23). It is patience instead of
anger, purity instead of lust, humility instead of
pride. Every time a believer resists temptation or
chooses forgiveness, the kingdom has advanced.
Thus, the first implication of Jesus' teaching is
deeply personal: the throne of God is established in
the heart that bows to Him in love and obedience.

2. **Daily Obedience:** Each act of submission to
   God's will is a sign of the kingdom's presence.
   Jesus declared, "Not everyone who says to me,
   'Lord, Lord,' will enter the kingdom of heaven, but
   only the one who does the will of my Father"
   (Matt. 7:21). The kingdom is not about mere
   confession but about lived obedience. This does
   not mean that obedience earns the kingdom, but
   that it reveals the kingdom's reality within us.
   Every choice becomes an opportunity to live under
   the King's reign: how we treat our families, how we
   handle money, how we speak of others, how we
   respond to suffering. Small acts of
   faithfulness—speaking truth, honoring
   commitments, serving quietly—become the seeds of

kingdom life. Obedience also requires surrender of self-will. Jesus Himself models this when He prays, "Not my will but yours be done" (Luke 22:42). Kingdom living, then, is not spectacular but steady—daily decisions, moment by moment, that align with the King's commands.

3. **Community Life:** Churches are outposts of the kingdom, living parables of God's reign in a broken world. The early church in Acts 2:42–47 displayed this reality: devoted to the apostles' teaching, to fellowship, to the breaking of bread, to prayer, and to generosity. The kingdom was seen not in wealth or political power but in love, reconciliation, and holiness. Every congregation is meant to be a miniature of the kingdom to come, a foretaste of heaven. The world should be able to look at the church and see a community shaped by forgiveness (Col. 3:13), unity (Eph. 4:3), and sacrificial service (John 13:14). Community life also challenges us to embody kingdom values across boundaries. In Christ, there is neither Jew nor Greek, slave nor free, male nor female (Gal. 3:28). The church is a family where cultural, social, and economic divisions are healed in the fellowship of the Spirit. To despise or neglect the community of believers is to despise the very place where the kingdom is meant to be seen most clearly.

4. **Mission to the World:** The kingdom is not hidden forever; what begins in secret grows until it fills the earth. Habakkuk 2:14 promises, "The earth will be filled with the knowledge of the glory of the

LORD as the waters cover the sea." Jesus' parables
echo this trajectory: what begins as a mustard seed
becomes a great tree (Matt. 13:31–32). Mission,
therefore, is the outward flow of the kingdom
within. Evangelism is not merely sharing
information but inviting others to bow to the King
and enter His reign. Acts of justice and mercy are
kingdom signs—feeding the hungry, caring for the
oppressed, welcoming the stranger. Jesus Himself
tied mission to kingdom proclamation: "This
gospel of the kingdom will be preached in the
whole world as a testimony to all nations" (Matt.
24:14). Mission is not optional but essential, for the
kingdom by nature expands. It is leaven working
through the dough, light shining in darkness, salt
permeating the earth. Every believer is a witness,
every church a base of kingdom advance, every act
of mercy a preview of the coming glory.

Summary. The kingdom of God is not an abstract idea
but a lived reality. It transforms the individual, demands
daily obedience, creates a new kind of community, and
fuels the church's mission to the world. It begins in the
heart but does not stay there; it flows outward in justice,
mercy, and love until the earth itself is renewed. The
practical implication of Jesus' words is this: every
believer, every day, in every place is called to live as a
citizen of the kingdom, carrying its presence within and
displaying its power among.

Reflection

As you meditate on Jesus' teaching that the kingdom of
God is both within and among us, consider these
extended questions and prompts. Let them guide your
prayer, journaling, and conversation with God and
others. Each is designed to help you not only understand
the kingdom intellectually but experience it personally
and practice it communally.

- **Personal Transformation:** How do you see the
  kingdom of God working within you today—in
  desires changed, sins resisted, love awakened? Can
  you name specific ways in which the Spirit has
  transformed your thoughts, emotions, or habits in
  recent weeks? Paul says, "It is God who works in
  you to will and to act in order to fulfill his good
  purpose" (Phil. 2:13). Where do you see evidence
  of His reign inside your heart? How might you
  celebrate these small but real victories as signs of
  the kingdom's advance?

- **Searching Outward vs. Inward:** Where might
  you be searching for God's reign "out there" while
  ignoring its call "in here"? Are you waiting for
  circumstances to change, for leaders to rise, or for
  visible proof of God's power, while neglecting the
  quiet work of repentance and obedience? Jesus said
  the kingdom does not come with observation but is
  within and among you (Luke 17:20–21). What
  would it mean to shift your focus from scanning
  the horizon to tending the soil of your own heart?

- **Nurturing Small Seeds:** What small seeds of
  the kingdom could you nurture right now through
  prayer, service, or forgiveness? Remember that
  Jesus likened the kingdom to a mustard seed and
  to yeast—tiny beginnings with enormous impact
  (Matt. 13:31–33). Could a single prayer for an
  enemy, a single act of kindness, or a single moment
  of generosity be the seed of something greater?
  How might God be inviting you to take small,
  faithful steps that will one day bear large fruit?

- **The Church as Kingdom Outpost:** How can
  your church embody the kingdom as a visible
  household of God in your community? Acts 2:42–47
  shows the early church living as a community of
  teaching, fellowship, prayer, generosity, and praise.
  What would it look like for your congregation to
  reflect those same kingdom values today? In what
  ways could hospitality, racial reconciliation, care
  for the poor, or bold witness make your local
  church a foretaste of God's reign? How might you
  personally contribute to that vision?

- **Suffering and Hope:** In what ways do suffering
  and waiting tempt you to doubt that the kingdom
  is real and present? Paul wrote, "We must go
  through many hardships to enter the kingdom of
  God" (Acts 14:22). How do trials cause you to
  question God's reign? Conversely, how might Jesus'
  words re-anchor your hope, reminding you that
  even in suffering the kingdom is advancing?
  Consider Romans 8:18: "Our present sufferings are
  not worth comparing with the glory that will be

revealed in us." What would it look like to endure
hardship as a citizen of the kingdom, confident of
its final fulfillment?

- **Kingdom Eyes:** Do you have eyes to see the
  kingdom at work in hidden places? Jesus often
  rebuked people for their inability to perceive
  spiritual reality (Matt. 13:13–15). Where might
  you need the Spirit to open your eyes to God's
  reign—in your workplace, in your family, in your
  neighborhood? How can you train yourself to look
  not only for dramatic events but for the quiet
  growth of God's work, like yeast spreading through
  dough?

- **Prayer as Participation:** How does prayer align
  you with the kingdom? When you pray, "Thy
  kingdom come," do you mean it? Do you expect
  God's will to be done in your own life first, before
  it is done in the world at large? Reflect on ways
  that consistent, focused prayer shapes you to desire
  the King's will above your own. Could you set
  aside regular time to intercede specifically for the
  spread of the kingdom in your home, church, city,
  and nations?

- **Obedience in the Ordinary:** How can everyday
  acts—honesty at work, kindness to a neighbor,
  patience with a child—become kingdom acts?
  Jesus taught that faithfulness in little things is
  great in God's eyes (Luke 16:10). Are you tempted
  to underestimate the significance of ordinary
  obedience? How might you reframe your daily
  routines as sacred opportunities to display God's

reign?

- **Justice and Mercy:** Since the kingdom is about
  righteousness, justice, and peace (Rom. 14:17),
  how might God be calling you to pursue these in
  your community? Are there people you could
  advocate for, serve, or defend as an expression of
  God's reign breaking into this world? Consider
  Micah 6:8: "What does the LORD require of you?
  To act justly, to love mercy, and to walk humbly
  with your God." How can you embody this verse as
  a kingdom citizen?

- **Living Between the Times:** How do you live in
  the tension of the "already and not yet"? The
  kingdom is already present but not yet fully
  revealed. How can you hold joy and longing
  together—rejoicing in what God has already done
  in you, yet yearning for Christ's return to make all
  things new? What practices—worship, lament,
  Eucharist, fasting—help you sustain faith in the
  tension of this in-between age?

- **Identity as a Kingdom Citizen:** Do you think
  of yourself primarily as a worker, parent, student,
  or citizen of a nation—or as a citizen of the
  kingdom of God (Phil. 3:20)? How would this
  identity reshape your priorities, your speech, and
  your use of time and money? What would change
  if you began every day reminding yourself: "I am
  an ambassador of Christ, a citizen of His kingdom,
  called to represent Him wherever I go"?

- **Witness to the World:** How does your life point

others to the reality of the kingdom? Jesus said, "You are the light of the world. A city set on a hill cannot be hidden" (Matt. 5:14). Do your neighbors, coworkers, and friends see in you a reflection of God's love, peace, and justice? What adjustments could you make so that your witness is clearer, your light brighter, your presence more evidently shaped by the King you serve?

- **Communal Discernment:** How can you and your community discern together where the kingdom is breaking in? The early church fasted and prayed to discern the Spirit's leading (Acts 13:2). Could your small group or congregation regularly ask, "Where do we see God's reign breaking through, and how can we join Him?" What might change if you measured church success not by numbers or programs but by signs of kingdom life—transformed hearts, reconciled relationships, bold witness, and justice pursued?

- **Future Orientation:** How does the promise of the kingdom's final revelation shape your daily choices? If you knew that every act of faithfulness is storing up treasure in heaven (Matt. 6:19–20), how would you live differently? How does the hope of a new heavens and new earth (2 Pet. 3:13) strengthen you to live faithfully now? What does it mean to live today in light of tomorrow's kingdom?

Take time to linger with these questions. Choose one or two each day to journal about or to bring before God in prayer. The kingdom of God is not distant or abstract; it

is already within you and among you. Let these
reflections train your heart to see, to trust, and to
participate in the reign of Christ in every area of life.

Chapter 4

The Authority of Words

Scripture Foundation

"The tongue has the power of life and death, and those who love it will eat its fruit." (Proverbs 18:21)

"Truly I tell you, if anyone says to this mountain, 'Go, throw yourself into the sea,' and does not doubt in their heart but believes that what they say will happen, it will be done for them." (Mark 11:23)

"Out of the overflow of the heart the mouth speaks." (Matthew 12:34)

"With the tongue we praise our Lord and Father, and with it we curse human beings, who have been made in God's likeness. Out of the same mouth come praise and cursing. My brothers and sisters, this should not be." (James 3:9–10)

"Let your conversation be always full of grace, seasoned

with salt, so that you may know how to answer everyone.''
(Colossians 4:6)
"Do not let any unwholesome talk come out of your mouths, but only what is helpful for building others up according to their needs, that it may benefit those who listen." (Ephesians 4:29)
"The words of the reckless pierce like swords, but the tongue of the wise brings healing." (Proverbs 12:18)

Themes

Made in God's image, our words carry profound weight. Just as God spoke creation into being, so too our speech has the ability to shape reality around us. Jesus emphasizes faith-filled words that align with God's will. Our speech can heal or wound, bless or curse, build faith or spread fear. To speak as children of Elohim is to choose words of life.

Words are never neutral. They either advance the kingdom of God or oppose it. When aligned with the Spirit, words heal, guide, and encourage. When aligned with the flesh, words deceive, divide, and destroy. The believer is called to steward speech as a holy trust, recognizing that careless words carry eternal consequences (Matt. 12:36–37).

Words as Creative Power

In Genesis 1, God speaks the universe into existence: "And God said, 'Let there be light,' and there was light." Creation itself testifies that words are not empty symbols but carriers of power. Humanity, created in His image, reflects this capacity. While our words do not create worlds ex nihilo, they do shape lives, communities, and futures.

Encouragement builds courage. Condemnation crushes hope. Words, once spoken, ripple outward in ways that cannot be recalled. Proverbs warns that "the tongue of the wise brings healing" but "the words of the reckless pierce like swords" (Prov. 12:18). The book of James compares the tongue to the rudder of a ship: small, but steering the entire course (James 3:4–5).

Jesus warns that we will give account for every careless word (Matt. 12:36). This is not hyperbole—it is recognition that words matter because words move hearts, and hearts move history. To bless is to release life; to curse is to sow death. The weight of our speech is a reflection of our dignity as image-bearers entrusted with creative capacity.

Words Reveal the Heart

Jesus teaches, "Out of the abundance of the heart the mouth speaks" (Matt. 12:34). Our words are mirrors of our inner life. Bitter words flow from bitterness; gracious words flow from grace. To discipline the tongue, we must

first examine the heart. Transformation of speech begins
with transformation of the soul.

Thus, the battle for pure speech is not fought only at the
lips but at the source—the wellspring of desires and
meditations within. David's prayer becomes ours: "Let
the words of my mouth and the meditation of my heart
be acceptable in Your sight, O LORD" (Ps. 19:14).

This truth humbles us. Complaints expose discontent.
Gossip exposes insecurity. Harsh words expose pride.
Conversely, gentle words reveal peace, thanksgiving
reveals faith, and encouragement reveals love. Speech is
the soul's echo.

Faith-Filled Confession

Jesus connects words to faith in Mark 11:23: mountains
move when faith and confession align. This is not
superstition or magical incantation, but the outworking
of trust in God's authority. When our words agree with
God's promises, they become instruments of His power.

Paul echoes this: "It is written: 'I believed; therefore I
have spoken.' Since we have that same spirit of faith, we
also believe and therefore speak" (2 Cor. 4:13).
Confession is not optional—it is how belief is activated
in speech.

Salvation itself is tied to confession: "If you declare with
your mouth, 'Jesus is Lord,' and believe in your heart
that God raised him from the dead, you will be saved"
(Rom. 10:9). Faith speaks. Silence in the face of truth

denies God's power, but confession unleashes it.

The Dangers of the Tongue

James devotes nearly a whole chapter to warning about the tongue (James 3:1–12). He compares it to a spark that can set a whole forest ablaze. Words wound reputations, destroy relationships, and sow division in the body of Christ.

Gossip, slander, grumbling, and deceit are not minor flaws but sins that oppose the kingdom. Jesus Himself said that by our words we will be justified, and by our words we will be condemned (Matt. 12:37). Paul urges, "Do not let any unwholesome talk come out of your mouths" (Eph. 4:29).

To misuse words is to misuse one of God's greatest gifts. Silence is sometimes wisdom; reckless speech is often folly. The enemy thrives on lies, half-truths, and accusations. Believers must resist becoming instruments of his work by allowing their tongues to be unbridled.

Blessing and Cursing

Scripture reminds us that words can invoke blessing or cursing. In Numbers 6:24–26, the priestly blessing invokes God's favor on His people, and to this day it remains a powerful benediction. Yet James laments that from the same mouth come both praise and cursing.

To curse another is to speak against one made in God's image, effectively striking at the Creator Himself. Proverbs 11:11 says, "Through the blessing of the upright a city is exalted, but by the mouth of the wicked it is destroyed."

The believer is called to break cycles of cursing and become an agent of blessing: "Bless those who persecute you; bless and do not curse" (Rom. 12:14). Jesus Himself blessed even from the cross: "Father, forgive them" (Luke 23:34). The choice to bless is the choice to partner with God's redemptive purposes.

The Ministry of Encouragement

Words not only avoid harm; they are called to actively build. Barnabas, whose name means "son of encouragement," models this ministry. Through words of affirmation and support, he nurtured Paul's ministry and encouraged the early church (Acts 11:23–24).

Encouragement is not flattery; it is Spirit-led speech that strengthens faith and stirs perseverance. Hebrews 3:13 commands, "Encourage one another daily, as long as it is called 'Today.'"

A silent church starves its members of courage. Words of encouragement create endurance in trials, joy in labor, and faith in hardship. To encourage is to partner with the Spirit in sustaining the body of Christ.

Speech in Prayer and Worship

Our words reach their highest authority in prayer and worship. Prayer is not babble into the void but dialogue with the King of kings. Worship is the language of heaven, aligning our words with eternal praise.

The Psalms show us that God receives words of lament, petition, thanksgiving, and exaltation. Jesus Himself prayed with words that shook heaven and earth (John 17). Paul and Silas prayed and sang hymns in prison, and the chains fell off (Acts 16:25–26).

The kingdom advances not by silence but by the proclamation of prayer and praise: "Through Jesus, therefore, let us continually offer to God a sacrifice of praise—the fruit of lips that openly profess his name" (Heb. 13:15).

Practical Applications

1. **Examine the Heart:** Since words reveal the heart, ask the Spirit to search your motives, fears, and desires. Pray Psalm 141:3, "Set a guard over my mouth, LORD; keep watch over the door of my lips."

2. **Practice Silence:** Restrain speech in moments of anger or temptation. Proverbs 10:19 reminds us, "When words are many, sin is not absent."

3. **Speak Scripture:** Let the Word of God shape your speech. Declare His promises out loud; use

Scripture in prayer and encouragement.

4. **Bless, Don't Curse:** Make it a discipline to bless others intentionally, even enemies. Speak life where others expect negativity.

5. **Encourage Daily:** Commit to offering daily words of encouragement. Look for opportunities to strengthen weary hearts with godly speech.

6. **Guard Against Gossip:** Refuse to participate in conversations that tear others down. Redirect toward prayer and support.

7. **Worship with Words:** Let your speech be filled with thanksgiving and praise, shaping your heart and community with joy.

Reflection

- Do your words more often create life or sow destruction?

- How can you align your speech with God's purposes this week?

- What "mountains" might move if you spoke in faith?

- Who in your life needs encouragement that only you can give?

- How can you practice blessing with your words, especially toward those who are difficult to love?

- What role does prayer and worship play in shaping the authority of your speech?

- When was the last time you confessed God's promises out loud? How did it shape your faith?

Chapter 5

Walking in Light

Scripture Foundation

"I am the light of the world. Whoever follows me will never walk in darkness, but will have the light of life." (John 8:12)

"For you were once darkness, but now you are light in the Lord. Live as children of light." (Ephesians 5:8)

"Your word is a lamp to my feet and a light to my path." (Psalm 119:105)

"You are the light of the world. A town built on a hill cannot be hidden." (Matthew 5:14)

"The path of the righteous is like the morning sun, shining ever brighter till the full light of day." (Proverbs 4:18)

"The light shines in the darkness, and the darkness has not overcome it." (John 1:5)

"Arise, shine, for your light has come, and the glory of the

LORD rises upon you." (Isaiah 60:1)

Themes

Jesus reveals himself as the light of the world, and those who follow him reflect that light. To walk in light is to embrace truth, compassion, and holiness. It means rejecting hypocrisy and secrecy, choosing transparency and integrity. As lamps are meant to shine, disciples are meant to live visibly in love.

Light not only guides our steps but exposes sin, heals wounds, and points others to Christ. Walking in light is not a private spirituality but a public witness; it is the transformation of character and community. Darkness deceives, isolates, and enslaves; light liberates, clarifies, and renews. Thus, to be children of light is both gift and calling: receiving illumination from Christ and radiating it into a world desperate for hope.

Christ the True Light

The Gospel of John opens with the declaration: "The true light that gives light to everyone was coming into the world" (John 1:9). Christ is not one light among many; He is the Light of the world. His light dispels the darkness of ignorance, sin, and despair.

To walk in light is first to acknowledge that we have no light of our own—we are moons, not suns. Our radiance comes only from reflecting Him. Just as the moon is

dark without the sun, so we are dark without Christ.
But when we abide in Him, His brilliance transforms our
weakness into witness.

Moreover, Christ's light reveals truth about God, about
ourselves, and about the world. Without Him we
stumble, but with Him we see clearly. He is both the
light who reveals and the life that renews.

From Darkness to Light

Paul reminds the Ephesians, "You were once darkness,
but now you are light in the Lord" (Eph. 5:8). Notice he
does not say merely that we were *in* darkness, but that
we *were* darkness itself. Sin is not only external acts but
an internal condition.

In Christ, that condition is reversed: we are not merely
placed in the light, but made light ourselves. This
transformation calls us to live as children of light,
producing "goodness, righteousness, and truth" (Eph.
5:9). The movement from darkness to light is a
fundamental shift in identity. As Peter writes, "God
called you out of darkness into his wonderful light" (1
Pet. 2:9).

Light as Guidance

Psalm 119:105 describes God's word as a lamp to our
feet. Light illuminates the path, exposing obstacles and
dangers. To walk in light means to live guided by

Scripture, directed by the Spirit, and attuned to God's will. Darkness confuses, but light clarifies.

Isaiah says, "Whether you turn to the right or to the left, your ears will hear a voice behind you, saying, 'This is the way; walk in it'" (Isa. 30:21). To live by light is to walk in obedience, moment by moment. The believer daily asks, "Am I stepping where the Word shines, or am I wandering into shadows?"

Light as Witness

Jesus calls His followers "the light of the world" (Matt. 5:14). This is not optional—it is identity. A lamp under a bowl is useless. To walk in light is to shine, to live in such a way that others see Christ's goodness and give glory to God (Matt. 5:16).

This witness is not about self-promotion but about transparency—our lives pointing beyond ourselves to the Light we reflect. As Paul writes, "You shine like stars in the sky as you hold firmly to the word of life" (Phil. 2:15–16). The darker the night, the brighter the stars shine.

Light as Exposure and Healing

Light not only guides but also exposes. "Everything exposed by the light becomes visible" (Eph. 5:13). The presence of Christ reveals hidden sin, hypocrisy, and injustice. For some, this exposure feels threatening; for others, it is the beginning of healing.

Just as sunlight disinfects and restores, so Christ's light cleanses what was hidden in shame. "If we walk in the light, as he is in the light, we have fellowship with one another, and the blood of Jesus... purifies us from all sin" (1 John 1:7). To walk in light is to welcome exposure before God, trusting that what He reveals, He heals.

Light and Spiritual Warfare

Darkness is not merely ignorance; it is opposition. Scripture depicts the dominion of darkness as resisting God's truth and enslaving humanity. Yet Christ's light overcomes: "He has rescued us from the dominion of darkness and brought us into the kingdom of the Son he loves" (Col. 1:13).

To walk in light is to participate in this victory, refusing compromise with sin and standing firm against lies. Spiritual warfare is not fought in secret but in the open clarity of Christ's light. Wherever the light shines, darkness flees.

Practical Applications

1. **Personal Integrity:** Live transparently, refusing to hide behind lies or hypocrisy. Let your words and actions match.

2. **Scriptural Guidance:** Daily engage God's Word as light for your path. Ask, "Am I walking where the lamp shines?"

3. **Community Example:** Shine as a witness in your family, workplace, and community. Your light is meant to be seen.

4. **Courage in Darkness:** Do not fear the shadows around you. A single candle dispels the dark; your faithful witness matters.

5. **Welcoming Exposure:** Invite God's Spirit to search you. Pray with David: "Search me, God, and know my heart" (Ps. 139:23).

6. **Healing Presence:** Be light for the hurting—encourage, comfort, and bring hope where despair lingers.

7. **Discernment:** Learn to distinguish between false lights and the true Light of Christ (2 Cor. 11:14).

8. **Prayer and Worship:** Let prayer and praise lift your heart into God's radiance, re-centering you in His presence.

Reflection

- What areas of your life remain in shadow, and how might Christ's light bring healing there?

- How could you become a clearer reflection of Christ's light this week—in words, actions, or attitudes?

- Who around you needs to see light shining through your example of love and truth?

- Do you welcome God's exposure of sin, or resist it? How might you learn to see exposure as the first step to healing?

- How might your church community shine more brightly as a city on a hill for the surrounding world?

- In what ways is light a comfort to you? In what ways is it a challenge?

- How does remembering Christ's final victory over darkness strengthen your courage to walk faithfully today?

Chapter 6

Love as Divine Nature

Scripture Foundation

"Dear friends, let us love one another, for love comes from God. Everyone who loves has been born of God and knows God. Whoever does not love does not know God, because God is love." (1 John 4:7–8)

"A new command I give you: Love one another. As I have loved you, so you must love one another. By this everyone will know that you are my disciples, if you love one another." (John 13:34–35)

"Above all, love each other deeply, because love covers over a multitude of sins." (1 Peter 4:8)

"Love is patient, love is kind. It does not envy, it does not boast, it is not proud." (1 Corinthians 13:4)

"Greater love has no one than this: to lay down one's life for one's friends." (John 15:13)

"But I tell you, love your enemies and pray for those who persecute you, that you may be children of your Father in heaven." (Matthew 5:44–45)

"And now these three remain: faith, hope and love. But the greatest of these is love." (1 Corinthians 13:13)

Themes

The essence of God's nature is love, and therefore the essence of our calling is love. To be in God's likeness is to love as He loves—sacrificially, unconditionally, faithfully. Jesus' new commandment to love one another is not optional; it is the defining mark of being God's children.

The cross is the supreme demonstration of love: "God demonstrates his own love for us in this: While we were still sinners, Christ died for us" (Rom. 5:8). Divine love is not abstract emotion but concrete action, rooted in God's initiative. To walk in divine love is to reflect the very heart of God to the world. Without love, even the greatest spiritual gifts are hollow (1 Cor. 13:1–3). Love is the currency of the kingdom and the law's fulfillment (Rom. 13:10).

God's Nature as Love

Love is not merely one attribute of God; it is His very essence. John declares, "God is love" (1 John 4:8). This means that all of God's actions—creation, covenant, discipline, salvation, judgment—flow from His love. Even

His justice is an expression of His love, for He defends the oppressed and confronts evil.

From Genesis to Revelation, Scripture reveals God's steadfast love (*hesed*) as covenantal loyalty: "The steadfast love of the LORD never ceases; his mercies never come to an end" (Lam. 3:22–23). The psalmist repeatedly declares, "His love endures forever" (Ps. 136). To know God is to encounter love at its purest, deepest, and most transformative source.

Any vision of God that neglects love distorts His character. Fear without love produces distortion; knowledge without love puffs up (1 Cor. 8:1). But love rightly reveals God's holiness, mercy, and truth in perfect harmony.

The Command of Christ

Jesus' command to love one another as He has loved us (John 13:34–35) raises the standard far beyond human affection. This is not mere tolerance or politeness but self-giving, sacrificial love.

Jesus washed His disciples' feet, showing that love serves. He laid down His life, showing that love sacrifices. He forgave His enemies, showing that love is merciful. He embraced the outcast, showing that love welcomes. Our love must mirror His, for by it the world recognizes His disciples.

This love extends to those who are hardest to love. "If you love those who love you, what reward will you get?"

Jesus asked (Matt. 5:46). Kingdom love exceeds human reciprocity; it embodies the Father's perfect love that shines on both the just and unjust.

The Cross as the Measure of Love

The cross stands as the ultimate measure of divine love. It was there that God gave His only Son so that we might live (John 3:16). Love is not sentimental feeling but costly action. Christ bore rejection, shame, and death so that we could be reconciled.

"Greater love has no one than this: to lay down one's life for one's friends" (John 15:13). Yet Christ's love went further: He laid down His life for His enemies (Rom. 5:10). To embrace divine love is to embrace a willingness to give, to forgive, and to serve even when it costs us dearly. The cross shapes how we define greatness, success, and faithfulness: not by power but by love poured out.

The Spirit's Work of Love

Love is not natural to the fallen heart; it is supernatural, produced by the Holy Spirit. "The fruit of the Spirit is love" (Gal. 5:22). To walk in love is to yield daily to the Spirit's work, allowing Him to soften hard hearts, heal wounds, and empower us to love beyond our capacity.

Paul prays that believers would be "rooted and established in love" and "grasp how wide and long and high and deep is the love of Christ" (Eph. 3:17–18). This depth of love is not humanly achievable; it must be revealed by the Spirit who pours God's love into our hearts (Rom. 5:5). Thus, divine love flows not from human effort alone but from the Spirit filling us with God's own life.

Love in the Church

The church is called to be a community of love where believers "carry each other's burdens" (Gal. 6:2), forgive one another (Col. 3:13), and build one another up (1 Thess. 5:11). When love reigns in the church, it becomes a foretaste of the kingdom.

Unity is preserved not by uniformity of opinion but by charity of heart. Love binds the body together: "Above all these put on love, which binds everything together in perfect harmony" (Col. 3:14).

The absence of love fractures witness: Paul rebuked the Corinthians for boasting in spiritual gifts without practicing love (1 Cor. 13). A loveless church may be doctrinally correct but spiritually bankrupt. Love is the bond of perfection and the mark by which the world recognizes Christ's presence.

Love in the World

To love as God loves extends beyond the household of faith. Jesus commands us to love even our enemies and pray for those who persecute us (Matt. 5:44). Divine love crosses boundaries of race, class, culture, and nationality. It defends the oppressed, cares for the poor, and seeks reconciliation.

The parable of the Good Samaritan (Luke 10:25–37) demonstrates that love recognizes no limits of neighborliness. True love sees need and responds, even at personal cost. John writes, "Let us not love with words or speech but with actions and in truth" (1 John 3:18).

Love in the world is evangelism in action. When the church practices radical generosity, forgiveness, and reconciliation, the watching world glimpses the reality of the gospel. Love embodied in deed authenticates love proclaimed in word.

Practical Applications

1. **Daily Surrender:** Begin each day by asking the Spirit to fill you with God's love, enabling you to see others as He sees them.

2. **Costly Service:** Look for opportunities to serve sacrificially, following Christ's example of foot-washing.

3. **Forgiveness:** Practice extending forgiveness as an act of divine love, remembering how God forgave you in Christ (Eph. 4:32).

4. **Words of Love:** Use speech to bless and build up rather than to wound or tear down (Eph. 4:29).

5. **Love in Action:** Express love through practical

deeds—hospitality, generosity, encouragement—that embody Christ's heart.

6. **Enemy Love:** Pray intentionally for those who hurt you, turning bitterness into intercession.

7. **Generous Giving:** Share resources with those in need, showing love in tangible provision (2 Cor. 9:7).

8. **Presence:** Be present with the lonely, the suffering, and the forgotten, embodying love through compassion.

Reflection

- How do you embody love in your daily interactions?

- What hinders you from loving more fully?

- How does divine love differ from worldly notions of affection?

- What would it look like to love someone difficult in your life with Christ-like love?

- In what ways could your church grow as a community marked more deeply by love?

- Where is God calling you to embody costly love in action, not just words?

- How might the Spirit be inviting you to expand the boundaries of your love—across cultures, classes, or even enemies?

Chapter 7

Justice and Mercy

Scripture Foundation

"Defend the weak and the fatherless; uphold the cause of the poor and the oppressed. Rescue the weak and the needy; deliver them from the hand of the wicked." (Psalm 82:3–4)

"He has shown you, O mortal, what is good. And what does the Lord require of you? To act justly and to love mercy and to walk humbly with your God." (Micah 6:8)

"The Spirit of the Lord is on me, because he has anointed me to proclaim good news to the poor. He has sent me to proclaim freedom for the prisoners and recovery of sight for the blind, to set the oppressed free." (Luke 4:18)

"Blessed are the merciful, for they will be shown mercy." (Matthew 5:7)

"Learn to do right; seek justice. Defend the oppressed.

Take up the cause of the fatherless; plead the case of the widow." (Isaiah 1:17)
"*Religion that God our Father accepts as pure and faultless is this: to look after orphans and widows in their distress and to keep oneself from being polluted by the world.*" (James 1:27)
"*For I, the LORD, love justice; I hate robbery and wrongdoing. In my faithfulness I will reward my people and make an everlasting covenant with them.*" (Isaiah 61:8)

Themes

Bearing God's image means carrying His concern for justice and mercy. Psalm 82 warns leaders against corrupt judgment, and Micah distills God's will into three actions: justice, mercy, humility. To live as Elohim is to defend the vulnerable, correct injustice, and extend compassion. Justice without mercy becomes harsh; mercy without justice becomes weak; together they reflect God's heart.

The prophets, the psalms, the teachings of Jesus, and the witness of the apostles all join in chorus: God's people must embody His righteousness by loving mercy and pursuing justice in every sphere of life. Injustice is never simply a political issue—it is a spiritual offense against God's image in humanity. Mercy is never weakness—it is the strength of God's love moving through His people. Justice and mercy together reveal God's kingdom breaking into a broken world.

God's Justice in Scripture

Justice is central to God's character. He is described as
"a God of justice" (Isa. 30:18), who "shows no partiality
and accepts no bribes" (Deut. 10:17). The prophets
repeatedly rebuke Israel not first for ritual failures but
for neglecting justice: "Woe to those who make unjust
laws, to those who issue oppressive decrees" (Isa. 10:1).
Amos cries out, "Let justice roll on like a river,
righteousness like a never-failing stream" (Amos 5:24).
Justice is not optional; it is covenantal faithfulness lived
out in community.

Justice in Scripture always carries relational weight. To
act justly means to protect the vulnerable and to treat
people rightly as bearers of God's image. It is not
abstract fairness but tangible righteousness lived out in
society. When rulers oppressed, prophets denounced
them. When widows or orphans were neglected, God's
wrath was stirred (Mal. 3:5). God's justice is restorative,
not merely punitive—it aims to set things right.

The Call to Mercy

Mercy is the tender counterpart to justice. God reveals
Himself to Moses as "the LORD, the compassionate and
gracious God, slow to anger, abounding in love and
faithfulness" (Exod. 34:6). Jesus' ministry embodied
mercy—healing lepers, forgiving sinners, touching the
unclean, feeding the hungry.

The Good Samaritan (Luke 10:25–37) illustrates mercy

that crosses cultural and social boundaries. Mercy is costly compassion, not passive sentiment. It stoops, sacrifices, and suffers with the hurting. The merciful are blessed, Jesus says, because in showing mercy they reflect the very heart of God and receive His mercy in return (Matt. 5:7).

Mercy also extends into forgiveness. Peter asked how many times he must forgive, and Jesus replied, "seventy times seven" (Matt. 18:22)—a call to limitless mercy. As God has forgiven us, so we must forgive (Col. 3:13). Mercy is both an act and a posture: a continual readiness to extend compassion to the undeserving.

Jesus as the Fulfillment of Justice and Mercy

In Jesus Christ, justice and mercy meet. On the cross, God's justice against sin and His mercy toward sinners are perfectly united. Paul writes that God is "just and the one who justifies those who have faith in Jesus" (Rom. 3:26). Justice demanded sin's penalty; mercy provided the substitute.

Jesus' inaugural sermon in Luke 4 announces His mission to bring both justice (freedom for the oppressed) and mercy (healing for the broken). His kingdom advances not through coercion but through love, not through oppression but through deliverance. He is the Good Shepherd who seeks the lost (mercy) and the righteous King who establishes equity (justice).

To follow Christ is to join Him in this mission. Believers are called to embody both justice and mercy in their homes, workplaces, churches, and communities. The gospel is never less than personal salvation, but it is always more: the restoration of God's order through Christ's reign.

Justice, Mercy, and Humility

Micah 6:8 ties justice and mercy to humility. Without humility, justice becomes self-righteousness and mercy becomes condescension. Walking humbly with God reminds us that we too are recipients of mercy, and therefore we cannot act with pride or arrogance toward others.

Humility keeps justice gentle and mercy strong. It acknowledges our limitations and prevents us from becoming what we oppose. It makes space for God's Spirit to work through us, rather than exalting our own efforts. Humility transforms justice into service and mercy into solidarity.

Practical Expressions of Justice and Mercy

1. **Defending the Vulnerable:** Stand with those who cannot stand for themselves—the poor, the fatherless, the widow, the stranger (Deut. 10:18–19).

2. **Practicing Forgiveness:** Extend mercy by releasing debts and offenses, remembering Christ's words, "Forgive, as you have been forgiven" (Col. 3:13).

3. **Generosity in Action:** Share resources with those in need, reflecting God's provision and compassion (2 Cor. 9:6–8).

4. **Speaking Truth:** Confront lies, exploitation, and oppression with courage, echoing the prophets' call for justice.

5. **Everyday Kindness:** Mercy is not only in great acts but in small daily choices—listening, comforting, encouraging, showing patience.

6. **Peacemaking:** Work to resolve conflict and reconcile broken relationships (Matt. 5:9).

7. **Advocacy:** Use influence, voice, or resources to speak for those silenced by systems of injustice.

8. **Hospitality:** Welcome strangers and outsiders, practicing mercy that creates belonging.

The Church as a Community of Justice and Mercy

The early church lived out this calling by caring for the poor, sharing possessions, and ensuring that widows were fed (Acts 6:1–7). James describes "pure religion" as caring for orphans and widows in their distress (James

1:27).

A church that ignores justice and mercy misrepresents the God it serves. A church that embodies them becomes a living testimony to the kingdom of God. When believers forgive debts, reconcile enemies, and provide for the needy, they proclaim a kingdom unlike the kingdoms of this world.

Throughout history, revivals have always been marked by both spiritual renewal and social transformation. Justice and mercy are not distractions from the gospel—they are evidence of it.

Eternal Perspective

Justice and mercy are not only present duties but eternal realities. Revelation 21 depicts a kingdom where every tear is wiped away and where righteousness dwells. Every act of justice now points forward to that day. Every act of mercy rehearses the eternal compassion of God.

The hope of eternity strengthens us in the present. Even when justice seems delayed or mercy is rejected, believers persevere, knowing God's kingdom will come in fullness. In the new creation, justice and mercy will kiss forever (Ps. 85:10). To live justly and mercifully now is to live in anticipation of that day.

Reflection

- Who around you is most in need of justice and mercy?

- How do you balance standing for truth with showing compassion?

- What role does humility play in living justly?

- Where in your community can you act as an advocate for the oppressed or a channel of mercy?

- How does the cross of Christ shape the way you hold justice and mercy together?

- In what ways can your church reflect God's concern for justice and mercy today?

- What small, daily practices can form you into a more just and merciful person?

Chapter 8

Prayer as Union

Scripture Foundation

"This, then, is how you should pray: 'Our Father in heaven, hallowed be your name, your kingdom come, your will be done, on earth as it is in heaven. Give us today our daily bread. And forgive us our debts, as we also have forgiven our debtors. And lead us not into temptation, but deliver us from the evil one.'" (Matthew 6:9–13)

"My prayer is not for them alone. I pray also for those who will believe in me through their message, that all of them may be one, Father, just as you are in me and I am in you. May they also be in us so that the world may believe that you have sent me." (John 17:20–21)

"Pray without ceasing." (1 Thessalonians 5:17)

"In the same way, the Spirit helps us in our weakness. We do not know what we ought to pray for, but the Spirit

himself intercedes for us through wordless groans."
(Romans 8:26)
"Do not be anxious about anything, but in every situation, by prayer and petition, with thanksgiving, present your requests to God. And the peace of God, which transcends all understanding, will guard your hearts and your minds in Christ Jesus." (Philippians 4:6–7)
"Devote yourselves to prayer, being watchful and thankful." (Colossians 4:2)
"The prayer of a righteous person is powerful and effective." (James 5:16)

Themes

Prayer is not just petition but participation. It is not merely the act of asking for things, but the entering of a holy dialogue in which the finite is caught up into the infinite, the created communes with the Creator, and the will of man is aligned with the will of God. Jesus models prayer as alignment with the Father's will and as intimate communion. In the Lord's Prayer we learn dependence ("Give us this day our daily bread"), forgiveness ("Forgive us our debts as we forgive our debtors"), and surrender ("Your will be done"). In John 17, we see Jesus' high priestly prayer that reveals His deepest longings for unity, sanctification, and glory for His disciples. Paul exhorts us to unceasing prayer (1 Thess. 5:17), a continual abiding in God's presence, showing that prayer is not bound to times or seasons, but is the ongoing breath of the soul.

Prayer is therefore both personal and communal, both inward and outward. Personally, it forms us into the likeness of Christ; communally, it binds the church into a family of intercession and thanksgiving. Prayer is a way of living in constant awareness of God's presence, letting His Spirit shape our desires and decisions. It is not only what we say but who we become through fellowship with the Father.

At its core, prayer unites heaven and earth. When we pray, God's kingdom draws near, His will is enacted in time and space, and His people are drawn into His mission. Prayer is not a religious exercise meant to ease the conscience, but a participation in God's ongoing work of redemption. Every whispered prayer, every cry of lament, every song of thanksgiving is woven into the eternal tapestry of God's plan. Prayer is where ordinary believers become co-laborers with God, lifting up the broken, standing against evil, and aligning with the Spirit's groaning for creation's renewal (Rom. 8:22–26).

Prayer as Communion with the Father

Prayer is first relational before it is functional. Jesus begins His model prayer with the words, "Our Father." This is revolutionary: the Almighty God is not approached as a distant monarch or impersonal force but as a loving Father who delights to hear His children. Communion, not transaction, is at the heart of prayer. Just as a child rests in the presence of a parent, so prayer is resting, trusting, and abiding in the Father's love.

This intimacy means prayer is not restricted to sacred spaces or formal words. Anywhere we are, the Father hears. Jonah cried out from the belly of the fish (Jonah 2:1–2), Hannah whispered her prayer in bitterness of soul (1 Sam. 1:10–13), and David poured out his heart on the run from Saul (Ps. 57:1). Even groans, tears, or silence can be prayer when offered in His presence (Rom. 8:26).

Communion makes prayer less about performance and more about presence—dwelling with the Father who already knows our needs before we ask (Matt. 6:8). True prayer is not about informing God but about transforming us through His nearness. In prayer we discover that God is not far off, but "in Him we live and move and have our being" (Acts 17:28).

Prayer as Alignment with God's Will

Prayer is not bending God to our desires but aligning ourselves with His purposes. The words "Your kingdom come, your will be done" (Matt. 6:10) are at the heart of all authentic prayer. Jesus models this alignment in Gethsemane when, sweating drops of blood, He submits: "Not my will but yours be done" (Luke 22:42). Prayer is not a tool for manipulating God; it is the posture of surrender that says, "Father, I trust Your wisdom above my own."

True prayer reshapes our longings, training our affections

to seek first the kingdom of God (Matt. 6:33). This means prayer is a school of desire. Left to ourselves, our petitions drift toward self-interest, comfort, or control. But in prayer, selfish impulses are refined, our limited vision expanded, and our fears calmed by God's sovereign goodness.

In prayer, human weakness meets divine wisdom. We learn to pray with open hands, releasing outcomes into God's care. Sometimes God says "yes," sometimes "no," and often "wait." In every case, prayer aligns us with His will, teaching us patience, trust, and obedience. The Psalms remind us that prayer holds lament and praise in the same breath, shaping our hearts into people who long not for our will, but for God's glory.

The Intercessory Heart of Jesus

John 17 reveals the union of Christ with the Father and His intercession for His people. Jesus prays for His disciples' protection ("Holy Father, protect them by the power of your name"), their sanctification ("Sanctify them by the truth"), and their unity ("that they may be one as we are one"). This prayer stretches forward through history: "I pray also for those who will believe in me through their message" (John 17:20). In other words, Jesus prayed for us long before we were born.

His intercession is not confined to the pages of Scripture. Even now, the risen Christ "always lives to intercede" for us (Heb. 7:25). He is our High Priest at the right hand of the Father, pleading for us when we stumble and fail.

When Peter was about to deny Him, Jesus said, "I have prayed for you, Simon, that your faith may not fail" (Luke 22:32). That same intercession extends to every believer.

This truth comforts us in weakness: even when we fail to pray, Jesus prays for us. His intercession ensures that our faith will not be extinguished. Prayer, then, is not only our speaking but our participation in the ongoing intercession of Christ. When we pray, we join our voices with the eternal Son who continually pleads our cause before the Father.

The Spirit's Role in Prayer

Prayer is not human effort alone. Paul reminds us in Romans 8:26 that the Spirit intercedes for us with groans too deep for words. When words fail, God Himself prays within us. The Spirit teaches us how to pray, stirs us to pray, and carries our prayers into perfect harmony with the Father's will.

The Spirit convicts us of sin, opens the Scriptures to us, awakens holy desires, and assures us of our adoption as God's children. "Because you are his sons, God sent the Spirit of his Son into our hearts, the Spirit who calls out, 'Abba, Father'" (Gal. 4:6). Thus, prayer is not simply initiated by us but prompted and sustained by the Spirit's indwelling presence.

To live in prayer is to live in the Spirit's stream, where weakness becomes strength and silence becomes worship.

When we cannot articulate the burden on our hearts, the Spirit turns sighs into petitions and tears into intercession. Prayer becomes a Trinitarian act: we pray to the Father, through the Son, in the Spirit, each Person of the Godhead drawing us deeper into divine communion.

Prayer as Ongoing Communion

Paul's command to "pray without ceasing" (1 Thess. 5:17) does not mean constant words but constant awareness. Prayer becomes the rhythm of life, woven into work, rest, and relationships. Brother Lawrence called this "practicing the presence of God"—a continuous turning of the heart toward Him in every task.

This ongoing communion turns ordinary life into sacred ground. Washing dishes, driving to work, or walking in nature can all become prayer when done in awareness of God's presence. Continuous prayer is not about length of speech but posture of the heart—the soul turned Godward in every circumstance.

The early church modeled this rhythm, devoting themselves "to the apostles' teaching and to fellowship, to the breaking of bread and to prayer" (Acts 2:42). This shows that prayer permeated their worship, their meals, their fellowship, and their mission. It was not confined to ritual but infused in every moment. To pray without ceasing is to live each day as an altar, each breath as an offering, and each moment as fellowship with God.

Prayer as Transformation

Prayer changes us. As Moses' face shone after being with God on Mount Sinai (Exod. 34:29), so prayer transforms us into His likeness. Paul writes, "We all, who with unveiled faces contemplate the Lord's glory, are being transformed into his image with ever-increasing glory" (2 Cor. 3:18). Prayer does not simply alter circumstances—it alters the one who prays.

Through prayer, bitterness is healed into forgiveness, anxiety into peace, fear into courage, and despair into hope. Over time, consistent prayer cultivates a Christ-shaped heart, one that beats in rhythm with His. Transformation through prayer is gradual but unmistakable, producing the fruit of the Spirit: love, joy, peace, patience, kindness, goodness, faithfulness, gentleness, and self-control (Gal. 5:22–23).

The desert fathers spoke of prayer as "fire in the heart," a slow but consuming flame that purifies the soul. Over years, prayer softens hardened hearts, enlarges compassion for enemies, deepens holiness, and builds resilience against temptation. In prayer we do not only ask for transformation—we become transformed. We begin to think God's thoughts, desire God's desires, and reflect God's character.

Practical Expressions of Union in Prayer

1. **Scripture Prayers:** Pray God's Word back to Him, allowing Scripture to shape desires.

2. **Silent Prayer:** Practice stillness before God, receiving His presence beyond words.

3. **Intercession:** Pray for others with the compassion of Christ, carrying their burdens before the Father.

4. **Confession and Forgiveness:** Keep short accounts with God, experiencing cleansing through honest prayer (1 John 1:9).

5. **Gratitude:** Begin and end each day with thanksgiving, cultivating awareness of God's goodness.

6. **Breath Prayers:** Simple phrases repeated in rhythm with breathing (e.g., "Lord Jesus Christ, have mercy on me").

7. **Corporate Prayer:** Join with fellow believers in agreement, for where two or three gather, Christ is present (Matt. 18:20).

8. **Listening Prayer:** Create space to hear God's whisper, not only to speak but to receive direction.

Reflection

- Do you see prayer more as asking or as union?

- How might your life change if prayer became ongoing communion?

- What prayers of Jesus inspire you most?

- In what ways can you allow the Spirit to pray through you when words fail?

- How could your church community grow in shared prayer as participation in God's mission?

- What distractions most hinder you from prayer, and how might you guard against them?

- How might prayer reshape your relationships—family, work, community—by aligning them with God's will?

Chapter 9

The Cross as Pattern

Scripture Foundation

"Whoever wants to be my disciple must deny themselves and take up their cross daily and follow me." (Luke 9:23)
"In your relationships with one another, have the same mindset as Christ Jesus: who, being in very nature God... humbled himself by becoming obedient to death—even death on a cross!" (Philippians 2:5–8)
"For the message of the cross is foolishness to those who are perishing, but to us who are being saved it is the power of God." (1 Corinthians 1:18)
"I have been crucified with Christ and I no longer live, but Christ lives in me." (Galatians 2:20)

Themes

The cross is not only the means of salvation but the
model of life. Jesus' humility and obedience reveal the
true nature of divine power: self-giving love. To follow
Him is to embrace sacrifice, service, and humility. The
cross is the pattern for how image-bearers live: laying
down life so that others may live. True discipleship is
cruciform—shaped by the cross in thought, attitude, and
action.

The Cross as God's Wisdom

Paul describes the cross as the wisdom of God that
confounds human pride (1 Cor. 1:18–25). The world
expects strength, wealth, or dominance to display divine
power. Instead, God chose the weakness of the cross to
overthrow sin and death. The cross unmasks human
arrogance and redefines wisdom as trust in God's
self-giving love. To follow the cross is to renounce
worldly measures of success and embrace God's strange
but saving wisdom.

The Cross as Self-Denial

Jesus' call to "deny yourself and take up your cross"
(Luke 9:23) confronts the human instinct for
self-preservation and self-exaltation. Self-denial is not
self-hatred but surrender—the yielding of control to God.

The disciple's daily rhythm is cruciform: dying to pride, greed, vengeance, and selfish ambition, so that Christ's life may shine through. Paul writes, "Those who belong to Christ Jesus have crucified the flesh with its passions and desires" (Gal. 5:24).

The Cross and Humility

Philippians 2 portrays Christ as the model of humility: though divine, He emptied Himself, taking the form of a servant, even to the point of death. This is not humiliation but holy descent. To live the cross-pattern is to resist entitlement, status-seeking, and pride. Greatness in God's kingdom is found in servanthood (Mark 10:43–45). Every act of humble service—washing feet, forgiving enemies, caring for the weak—mirrors the humility of Christ.

The Cross as Love in Action

At its heart, the cross is love made visible. "Greater love has no one than this: to lay down one's life for one's friends" (John 15:13). Love is not sentiment but sacrifice. The disciple learns that to follow Christ is to embody love that costs—time, energy, comfort, even reputation. The cross is love that endures rejection and still forgives, love that bears suffering and still serves.

The Cross and Suffering

The way of the cross includes suffering, but suffering in union with Christ is never wasted. Peter reminds believers, "Do not be surprised at the fiery ordeal that has come on you... but rejoice inasmuch as you participate in the sufferings of Christ" (1 Pet. 4:12–13). To take up the cross is to accept that hardship will accompany obedience, yet in that hardship God refines faith and reveals His presence.

The Cross and Resurrection Hope

The cross is never the end; it leads to resurrection. Jesus endured the cross "for the joy set before him" (Heb. 12:2). For the believer, every act of self-denial, every sacrifice in love, is sown into the soil of resurrection hope. To embrace the cross is to trust that loss in Christ becomes gain, and death in Christ becomes life. The cross shapes us for the glory that awaits.

Practical Applications

1. **Daily Denial:** Practice saying "no" to self-centered impulses and "yes" to God's will.

2. **Serve in Hidden Ways:** Look for opportunities to serve without recognition, imitating Christ's humility.

3. **Forgive Offenses:** Embrace the costly love of the cross by extending forgiveness even when it hurts.

4. **Embrace Weakness:** Trust that God's power is made perfect in weakness (2 Cor. 12:9).

Chapter 10

Resurrection Life

Scripture Foundation

"Jesus said to her, 'I am the resurrection and the life. The one who believes in me will live, even though they die; and whoever lives by believing in me will never die."' (John 11:25–26)

"We were therefore buried with him through baptism into death in order that, just as Christ was raised from the dead through the glory of the Father, we too may live a new life." (Romans 6:4)

"If the Spirit of him who raised Jesus from the dead is living in you, he who raised Christ from the dead will also give life to your mortal bodies because of his Spirit who lives in you." (Romans 8:11)

"Praise be to the God and Father of our Lord Jesus Christ! In his great mercy he has given us new birth into

a living hope through the resurrection of Jesus Christ from the dead." (1 Peter 1:3)

"The last enemy to be destroyed is death." (1 Corinthians 15:26)

"But Christ has indeed been raised from the dead, the firstfruits of those who have fallen asleep." (1 Corinthians 15:20)

"For since death came through a man, the resurrection of the dead comes also through a man. For as in Adam all die, so in Christ all will be made alive." (1 Corinthians 15:21–22)

"For the perishable must clothe itself with the imperishable, and the mortal with immortality. When the perishable has been clothed with the imperishable, and the mortal with immortality, then the saying that is written will come true: 'Death has been swallowed up in victory.'" (1 Corinthians 15:53–54)

"Blessed and holy are those who share in the first resurrection. The second death has no power over them, but they will be priests of God and of Christ and will reign with him for a thousand years." (Revelation 20:6)

Themes

Resurrection is not only a distant promise that awaits believers at the end of history but a present reality that reshapes every aspect of life here and now. When the New Testament proclaims, "Christ is risen," it does not merely speak of an event in the past or of a vague hope for the future, but of a transforming power alive in the present. Jesus' victory over death means that believers live in newness now—freedom from sin's dominion, empowerment by the Spirit, and the confident anticipation of eternal life. Resurrection life is marked by joy that cannot be extinguished by sorrow, courage that cannot be broken by fear, and hope that no earthly disappointment can erase. It is a life rooted in deep and abiding union with Christ: buried with Him in death, raised with Him into glory, and sustained by His presence through the Holy Spirit.

Resurrection as Transformation of Identity

This reality transforms the very identity of the Christian. Paul reminds us, "If anyone is in Christ, the new creation has come: the old has gone, the new is here!" (2 Cor. 5:17). Resurrection shifts how we define ourselves. We are no longer identified by sin, shame, or fear of death, but by the risen Christ who indwells us. The chains of condemnation are shattered; the fear of death is broken. As Paul exclaims, "Death has been swallowed up in victory" (1 Cor. 15:54). Believers now walk in the dignity of sons and daughters of God, clothed with resurrection life as a present possession.

Resurrection as Transformation of Mission

Resurrection also transforms our mission. We do not merely survive in a fallen world; we proclaim the good news that death has been defeated, sin's grip has been broken, and new life is available through Christ. Every act of evangelism is an announcement of resurrection reality. Peter, who once trembled before a servant girl, stood boldly at Pentecost and declared, "God has raised this Jesus to life, and we are all witnesses of it" (Acts 2:32). The resurrection turns cowards into heralds, sufferers into servants, wanderers into witnesses.

Resurrection and Suffering

Resurrection further transforms our understanding of suffering. Trials and hardships are no longer meaningless accidents but the birth pangs of glory. Paul writes, "I consider that our present sufferings are not worth comparing with the glory that will be revealed in us" (Rom. 8:18). Suffering, when joined to Christ, becomes participation in His death and anticipation of His resurrection. The Christian endures with hope because the cross was not the end for Jesus, and it will not be the end for us. Even in grief, we "do not grieve like the rest of mankind, who have no hope" (1 Thess. 4:13), for resurrection assures us that every loss will be restored in God's kingdom.

Resurrection as a Communal Reality

Resurrection also carries a communal dimension. Believers share in the life of the risen Christ together as His body, the church. Paul describes us as being "raised up with Christ and seated with him in the heavenly realms" (Eph. 2:6). This resurrection binding creates a community of hope, called to embody new-creation life in the midst of a broken world. Our corporate worship becomes a foretaste of the great resurrection feast, our fellowship a testimony that death's isolation has been overcome. Every gathering of believers is a miniature Easter morning, a living testimony that Christ is alive and that His life pulses through His body.

The resurrection makes our gatherings foretastes of the kingdom where every tear will be wiped away (Rev. 21:4). This is why the early church met on the first day of the week, the day of resurrection, to break bread and celebrate the victory of Christ. Resurrection is not only personal but corporate, not only present but cosmic—the beginning of the renewal of all things. Paul insists that creation itself "waits in eager expectation for the children of God to be revealed" (Rom. 8:19). Our resurrection is not isolated but bound to the liberation of the cosmos itself.

Resurrection and Perseverance

Finally, resurrection is a call to perseverance. Because Christ is risen, our labor in the Lord is not in vain (1 Cor. 15:58). Every act of service, every prayer offered in faith, every step of obedience, and every sacrifice of love participates in resurrection life now and will echo into eternity. Resurrection means nothing is wasted. Even the smallest deed, when done in Christ, carries eternal weight. Paul can exhort believers not to grow weary in doing good (Gal. 6:9) because resurrection assures us that a harvest is guaranteed.

The Resurrection of Christ as the Center of Faith

Paul declares with uncompromising clarity, "If Christ has not been raised, your faith is futile; you are still in your sins" (1 Cor. 15:17). The resurrection is not an optional doctrine but the cornerstone of Christian faith. Without resurrection, Christianity collapses into moralism and empty ritual. With resurrection, it becomes the living hope of humanity. It validates Christ's claims, confirms the power of His cross, and inaugurates the new creation. Everything rests on the reality that the tomb is empty.

Resurrection as Vindication of Jesus

The resurrection affirms that Jesus is who He claimed to be—the Son of God and Lord over all. His miracles, teachings, and even His sacrificial death would remain incomplete without the vindication of resurrection. Paul writes that Jesus "was appointed the Son of God in power by his resurrection from the dead" (Rom. 1:4). The empty tomb is heaven's declaration that Jesus is not merely a prophet but the eternal Son. The resurrection is God's divine stamp of approval on the life and work of Christ.

Resurrection as Victory over Death and Powers

The empty tomb declares victory not only over physical death but over sin, Satan, and all spiritual powers. Colossians 2:15 declares that through the cross and resurrection, Christ "disarmed the powers and authorities, making a public spectacle of them, triumphing over them by the cross." Death, once humanity's great tyrant, has been dethroned. The resurrection proclaims liberty to captives and light to those in darkness. This victory redefines death itself, not as an end but as a doorway into eternal communion with God.

The Apostolic Witness

This central truth is the ground of Christian proclamation. The apostles consistently preached not merely "Jesus crucified" but "Jesus crucified and risen" (Acts 2:24; Acts 4:10; Acts 17:31). Peter proclaimed, "God raised him from the dead. . . because it was impossible for death to keep its hold on him" (Acts 2:24). Paul declared to the Athenians that God "has set a day when he will judge the world with justice by the man he has appointed. He has given proof of this to everyone by raising him from the dead" (Acts 17:31). The resurrection was not a marginal note; it was the central theme. Without resurrection, there would be no gospel, no church, and no hope.

Resurrection as the Reorientation of History

Furthermore, the resurrection reorients all of history. It marks the dawn of God's new creation. Paul calls Christ "the firstfruits of those who have fallen asleep" (1 Cor. 15:20), meaning His resurrection guarantees ours. Just as the first sheaf of harvest promises the full crop to come, so Christ's rising assures that His people will follow. The empty tomb is not only Christ's vindication but our destiny. As Jesus Himself declared, "Because I live, you also will live" (John 14:19). Resurrection reframes time itself—there is a "before Easter" and an "after Easter" in the story of the world.

Theological Centrality

To remove the resurrection from Christian faith is to tear the heart out of the gospel itself. Without it, Christ is a martyr but not a Savior; faith is a sentiment but not a power; hope is a dream but not a certainty. With it, the gospel becomes the announcement that life has triumphed over death, truth over falsehood, righteousness over sin, and love over hatred. It is the fulcrum of salvation history. As Augustine said, "We are an Easter people, and Alleluia is our song."

Resurrection as New Birth

Peter calls it a "new birth into a living hope" (1 Pet.
1:3). Resurrection is more than resuscitation—it is
transformation. Believers are not merely improved but
reborn. The old life is crucified; the new life is
Spirit-filled and eternal. This is why baptism is linked to
resurrection: it symbolizes dying with Christ and rising
into His new life (Rom. 6:4).

This new birth changes our status before God. We are
no longer slaves but children; no longer condemned but
justified; no longer dead in sin but alive in Christ (Eph.
2:4–6). The Spirit who raised Jesus now breathes into us
a new identity, making us citizens of heaven (Phil. 3:20).
Our lives are not simply patched up—they are recreated.

Resurrection new birth also reshapes how we live in the
present. Because we have been raised with Christ, Paul
exhorts us to "set your hearts on things above" (Col.
3:1). Our affections, priorities, and values are redirected
toward the eternal. We no longer live under the
dominion of sin, for "sin shall no longer be your master,
because you are not under the law, but under grace"
(Rom. 6:14). This freedom empowers us to walk in
holiness, love, and joy.

Finally, resurrection new birth equips us with living hope.
Unlike fragile optimism based on circumstances, this
hope is anchored in the unshakable reality of the risen
Christ. Even in suffering, believers rejoice because their
hope is imperishable, undefiled, and unfading, "kept in
heaven" (1 Pet. 1:4). Thus, resurrection as new birth is

both present empowerment and future assurance, a truth
that sustains endurance until we see Christ face to face.

Resurrection and the Spirit's Power

The resurrection of Jesus is not simply an isolated event
in history; it is the inauguration of a new era, one
empowered and sustained by the Holy Spirit. Paul
declares with breathtaking clarity: "If the Spirit of him
who raised Jesus from the dead is living in you, he who
raised Christ from the dead will also give life to your
mortal bodies" (Rom. 8:11). This means the same Spirit
who called Christ forth from the tomb now resides within
the believer, animating them with the very power of God.
Resurrection is not merely remembered, it is embodied.
It is not a distant doctrine, but a lived reality, for the
Spirit mediates the life of the risen Christ to His people.

The Spirit as the Agent of Resurrection

Throughout Scripture, the Spirit is depicted as the
breath of God bringing life out of death. In creation, the
Spirit hovered over the waters (Gen. 1:2). In Ezekiel's
valley of dry bones, the Spirit breathed life into slain
warriors, raising them to their feet (Ezek. 37:1–14). At
Pentecost, tongues of fire filled the church with new
vitality (Acts 2:1–4). Each of these moments culminates
in the resurrection, where the Spirit raised Christ in
power and now applies that same victory to His body,

the church. The Spirit who breathes life into dry bones is the Spirit who breathes resurrection into weary souls.

The Spirit and Victory Over Sin

The resurrection life empowered by the Spirit brings freedom from the tyranny of sin. Paul writes, "For sin shall no longer be your master, because you are not under the law, but under grace" (Rom. 6:14). Sin's dominion is broken not by human willpower but by the indwelling Spirit, who applies Christ's finished work. Every act of holiness, every victory over temptation, every whisper of repentance is evidence of resurrection life at work. Believers no longer fight alone; the very Spirit who conquered death fights within them.

The Spirit and Bold Witness

Resurrection power also emboldens believers for mission. Before Pentecost, the disciples cowered in fear. After Pentecost, they spoke with courage, proclaiming Christ crucified and risen in the face of persecution. Resurrection power turns trembling lips into proclaiming voices. The Spirit empowers ordinary men and women to be extraordinary witnesses, fulfilling Jesus' promise: "You will receive power when the Holy Spirit comes on you; and you will be my witnesses" (Acts 1:8). Every testimony, every act of witness, every proclamation of the gospel is resurrection life expressed through the Spirit.

Resurrection   and   Daily Transformation

The resurrection is not reserved for the last day; it invades the present with transforming power. Paul insists, "If anyone is in Christ, the new creation has come: the old has gone, the new is here!" (2 Cor. 5:17). This declaration means resurrection is not theoretical but practical, not abstract but tangible. It reshapes priorities, renews minds, and reorients desires.

The Renewing of the Mind

Paul exhorts believers to "be transformed by the renewing of your mind" (Rom. 12:2). Resurrection life rewires the very patterns of thought. Where bitterness once ruled, forgiveness takes its place; where greed enslaved, generosity blossoms; where fear prevailed, courage abounds. The risen Christ not only changes behavior but transforms identity from within. Every reoriented desire, every healed memory, every redirected longing is evidence of resurrection power reshaping the inner life.

The Fruit of Resurrection Life

Resurrection life manifests outwardly through the fruit of the Spirit: "love, joy, peace, patience, kindness, goodness, faithfulness, gentleness, and self-control" (Gal. 5:22–23). These are not moral improvements achieved by effort but divine realities produced by resurrection power within. They demonstrate that Christ's victory is not only cosmic but personal. Forgiveness replaces vengeance, joy supplants despair, and courage replaces cowardice. Resurrection is not only something we wait for—it is something we wear daily.

Examples in Daily Living

Resurrection life appears in countless ways:

- A parent extends patience in the midst of exhaustion.

- A businessperson acts with integrity rather than exploitation.

- A believer forgives an old wound that once poisoned the heart.

- A church shares its resources generously with the poor.

Each of these small victories reveals resurrection at work. They are living testimonies that the risen Christ is not confined to the past or future but is alive here and now.

Resurrection and Suffering

Resurrection radically redefines suffering. Paul writes, "We always carry around in our body the death of Jesus, so that the life of Jesus may also be revealed in our body" (2 Cor. 4:10). To the world, suffering appears as defeat, but in Christ, suffering becomes seedbed for glory. Just as Christ's death gave way to victory, so too the believer's trials become opportunities for resurrection power to shine.

Hope in the Midst of Pain

Hope does not deny pain but transforms it. Christian hope looks squarely at suffering, acknowledges its reality, and yet declares with Paul, "Our present sufferings are not worth comparing with the glory that will be revealed in us" (Rom. 8:18). Suffering is not meaningless; it is pregnant with resurrection promise. Every tear anticipates joy, every trial anticipates vindication, every cross anticipates a crown.

Suffering as Participation with Christ

Suffering also draws believers into deeper fellowship with Christ. Paul longed to "know Christ—yes, to know the power of his resurrection and participation in his sufferings" (Phil. 3:10). To suffer as a Christian is not to be abandoned but to walk the same path as the Savior. The cross precedes the crown. Trials are not evidence of God's absence but arenas for His presence, proving that the power that raised Christ will sustain His people.

Resurrection Hope and the Future

Resurrection points us toward the consummation of God's kingdom: the resurrection of the body and the renewal of all creation. Paul assures us, "The trumpet will sound, the dead will be raised imperishable, and we will be changed" (1 Cor. 15:52).

The Future Resurrection of the Body

Unlike pagan philosophies that despise the body, Scripture affirms the redemption of the whole person. The believer's destiny is not escape from the material world but its transformation. Paul teaches that "the perishable must clothe itself with the imperishable" (1 Cor. 15:53). Our future bodies will be imperishable, glorious, powerful, and spiritual (1 Cor. 15:42–44). The risen Christ is the "firstfruits" (1 Cor. 15:20)—His resurrection guarantees ours. Just as He rose in a glorified body, so shall we.

The Renewal of Creation

The scope of resurrection is cosmic. Paul declares that creation itself "will be liberated from its bondage to decay and brought into the freedom and glory of the children of God" (Rom. 8:21). The resurrection of Jesus is the down payment of a renewed creation where righteousness dwells, where every tear is wiped away (Rev. 21:4), and where death shall be no more. Believers do not await escape from the world but its transfiguration.

Practical Applications

1. **Live Free from Sin:** Embrace resurrection life by walking in the freedom Christ purchased. "Count yourselves dead to sin but alive to God in Christ Jesus" (Rom. 6:11). Do not return to chains that have been broken.

2. **Walk in the Spirit:** Depend daily on the Spirit's power to strengthen, guide, and transform. Ask the Spirit to fill you afresh, knowing that His indwelling presence is resurrection power within.

3. **Practice Hope:** Cultivate habits of hope—gratitude, prayer, worship—that lift your vision beyond present trials to the eternal promises of God. Hope becomes a discipline as well as a gift.

4. **Embody Joy:** Let joy be your testimony, a fruit of resurrection life that cannot be stolen by circumstances. Joy is not shallow happiness but a deep current flowing from the empty tomb.

5. **Endure Suffering with Faith:** See trials as places where resurrection power can be revealed through perseverance and witness. Every cross borne in faith becomes a testimony of victory.

Reflection

- How do you experience resurrection power in your daily life?

- What does "new life" mean in practical terms for you?

- How does resurrection reshape your view of death and suffering?

- In what ways can you be a sign of resurrection hope to others?

- How does the Spirit's presence in you testify that resurrection life is real and active now?

- What fears lose their grip when you remember that Christ has risen and you are risen with Him?

- How can your church embody resurrection life as a community of joy, courage, and witness?

- What habits, patterns, or sins do you need to leave in the tomb, so that you may walk in newness of life?

Chapter 11

Becoming What You Are

Scripture Foundation

"And just as we have borne the image of the earthly man, so shall we bear the image of the heavenly man." (1 Corinthians 15:49)

"And we all, who with unveiled faces contemplate the Lord's glory, are being transformed into his image with ever-increasing glory, which comes from the Lord, who is the Spirit." (2 Corinthians 3:18)

"Beloved, now we are children of God, and what we will be has not yet been revealed. But we know that when Christ appears, we shall be like him, for we shall see him as he is." (1 John 3:2)

135

"For those God foreknew he also predestined to be conformed to the image of his Son." (Romans 8:29)

Themes

The Christian journey is a process of transformation—becoming what we already are in Christ. Though marred by sin, the image is being restored. We are moving from glory to glory, shaped into the likeness of the Son. The end goal is nothing less than bearing the image of the heavenly man fully. The Christian life is both "already" and "not yet": already made new in Christ, yet still being conformed until the day of resurrection.

The Tension of the Already and the Not Yet

Paul speaks of believers as already new creations (2 Cor. 5:17), yet also as people who are "being transformed" (2 Cor. 3:18). We live in tension: justified and declared righteous, yet still being sanctified; children of God already, yet waiting to see Christ and be like Him (1 John 3:2). This tension teaches us patience and humility as we trust God's ongoing work in us.

The Work of the Spirit in Transformation

Transformation is not achieved by sheer effort but by the Spirit's power. Paul says we are being transformed "from glory to glory" by the Spirit (2 Cor. 3:18). The Spirit convicts, renews, and empowers, gradually conforming us to Christ's image. Spiritual disciplines—prayer, Scripture, worship—are not ends in themselves but channels through which the Spirit reshapes us.

Conformed to Christ, the Heavenly Man

Jesus is described as the "heavenly man," the pattern and goal of our transformation (1 Cor. 15:49). As Adam represented fallen humanity, so Christ represents redeemed humanity. To bear the image of the heavenly man is to live in holiness, love, and resurrection life. This conformity is God's eternal plan (Rom. 8:29), ensuring that Christ will be the "firstborn among many brothers and sisters."

Transformation Through Suffering

Often, God uses suffering as a tool of transformation. Paul writes, "We also glory in our sufferings, because we know that suffering produces perseverance; perseverance, character; and character, hope" (Rom. 5:3–4). Hardship strips away self-reliance and deepens Christlike character. Trials, rather than derailing transformation, often accelerate it, chiseling us into the likeness of the Son.

Transformation as Hope of Glory

The promise of transformation is future-oriented as well: "When Christ appears, we shall be like him" (1 John 3:2). Our ultimate destiny is glorification—sharing in the glory of the risen Christ. This hope sustains endurance and shapes daily living. Knowing that we will bear the image of the heavenly man fully encourages us to live now in anticipation of that reality.

Practical Applications

1. **Daily Renewal:** Invite the Spirit to transform your mind each day (Rom. 12:2).

2. **Practice Patience:** Accept that transformation is a lifelong journey, not an instant change.

3. **Embrace Suffering:** See trials as opportunities for growth in Christlikeness.

4. **Christlike Imitation:** Ask in every decision, "How would Christ act in this situation?"

5. **Hopeful Living:** Let the promise of future glory strengthen present faithfulness.

Reflection

- Where do you see God's transforming work in your life right now?

- How does the promise of bearing Christ's image encourage you?

- What practices help you open yourself to God's transforming Spirit?

- How does living in the "already and not yet" tension change the way you see your struggles?

- What does it mean for you to bear the image of the heavenly man today?

Workbook: Daily and Weekly Practices

Daily Practices

- **Morning Prayer of Surrender:** Begin the day with a brief prayer patterned after Luke 22:42 and Romans 12:1—"Father, I offer my body as a living sacrifice. Not my will, but Yours be done. Order my steps in Your word."

- **Scripture First:** Read a short passage (e.g., a Psalm, a Gospel paragraph, or a Proverbs verse). Linger over one phrase and carry it as a refrain (Joshua 1:8).

- **Gratitude at the Table:** Before each meal, give thanks (1 Thess. 5:18). Name one specific gift from God's hand today (James 1:17).

- **Blessing with Your Work:** As you begin work, pray Colossians 3:23–24. Name one person you'll

140

serve through your labor and ask God to bless
them.

- **Intercession Pulse:** Set two small "alarms."
When they ring, pause for sixty seconds to pray for
someone in need (1 Tim. 2:1).

- **Evening Examen:** With Psalm 139:23–24, review
the day: Where did I sense God's presence? Where
did I resist grace? Confess, give thanks, and
receive peace (1 John 1:9).

Weekly Practices

- **Lord's Day Worship:** Gather with the church
(Heb. 10:24–25). Receive Word and Table if
available. Rest from striving (Ex. 20:8–11; Matt.
11:28–30).

- **Sabbath Simplicity:** Choose one block of time to
cease from buying, scrolling, or hustling. Practice
holy leisure—walk, sing, or share a simple meal
(Mark 2:27).

- **Generosity Rhythm:** Set aside your first and
best for the Lord (Prov. 3:9–10; 2 Cor. 9:6–8).
Give to your local church and one person or family
in quiet need (Matt. 6:3–4).

- **Journaling with the Word:** Review the week
with three headings: *Mercies Received, Sins
Confessed, Next Faithful Step.* Anchor each with a
verse.

- **Reconciliation Check:** Ask: Is anyone I need to

forgive or seek forgiveness from? Take one humble
step (Matt. 5:23–24; Eph. 4:32).

- **Household Liturgy:** Pray aloud the Lord's
Prayer together (Matt. 6:9–13). If alone, call a
friend and pray for one another (James 5:16).

Selected Readings and Sources

Holy Scripture (Primary Source)

- *The Holy Bible* — Old and New Testaments as the authoritative Word of God (2 Tim. 3:16–17). Key anchors for this book: Genesis 1–3; Psalms; Isaiah; the Gospels; Acts; Romans; Ephesians; 1 Corinthians 12–13; Hebrews; 1 John.

Creeds and Catechesis

- *The Apostles' Creed* and *Nicene Creed* — Concise summaries of the Christian faith, confessing the Triune God and the Lordship of Christ.

- *Heidelberg Catechism / Westminster Shorter Catechism* — Pastoral instruction on doctrine and discipleship.

- *Catechism of the Catholic Church* — A comprehensive articulation of Christian doctrine and moral life.

Classics of Christian Devotion

- Augustine, *Confessions* — Restless hearts finding rest in God; grace and desire.

- Thomas à Kempis, *The Imitation of Christ* — Humility, hiddenness, and union with Jesus.

- Brother Lawrence, *The Practice of the Presence of God* — Prayer in the ordinary; unceasing communion.

- Teresa of Ávila, *Interior Castle* — Prayer as journey into the soul's dwelling with God.

- John of the Cross, *Dark Night of the Soul* — Purification, detachment, and love's maturity.

Doctrine, Ethics, and Spiritual Formation

- Athanasius, *On the Incarnation* — The Word made flesh for our salvation.

- Thomas Aquinas, *Summa Theologiae* (selected) — Virtue, charity, and the moral life ordered to God.

- John Calvin, *Institutes of the Christian Religion* (selected) — God's sovereignty, grace, and the

Christian life.

- John Wesley, *Sermons* & *Plain Account of Christian Perfection* — Holiness of heart and life.

- C. S. Lewis, *Mere Christianity* — Mere core orthodoxy and moral vision; *The Great Divorce* — sanctification imagined.

- Dietrich Bonhoeffer, *Discipleship* — Costly grace and obedience to Christ.

- Dallas Willard, *The Divine Conspiracy* — Apprenticeship to Jesus and the kingdom life.

- N. T. Wright, *After You Believe* / *Simply Christian* — Virtue, hope, and the story of God.

- Henri Nouwen, *The Return of the Prodigal Son* — Identity as beloved sons and daughters.

- Eugene Peterson, *A Long Obedience in the Same Direction* — Psalms of Ascent and resilient discipleship.

Justice, Mercy, and Public Life

- Ron Sider, *Rich Christians in an Age of Hunger* — Biblical economics of generosity and justice.

- Timothy Keller, *Generous Justice* — Mercy and justice as fruits of the gospel.

- Robert Lupton, *Toxic Charity* and Corbett & Fikkert, *When Helping Hurts* — Wise compassion that restores dignity.

- Catholic Social Teaching (*Rerum Novarum, Centesimus Annus*) — Work, family, and the common good.

On Prayer and Worship

- *The Book of Common Prayer* — Forms and collects that train the heart in Scripture-shaped prayer.

- Andrew Murray, *With Christ in the School of Prayer* — Persevering, faith-filled intercession.

- Richard Foster, *Celebration of Discipline* — Classic disciplines (prayer, fasting, service, confession, worship).

Glossary of Key Terms

Sanctification: The Spirit's ongoing work conforming believers to the image of Christ (Rom. 8:29; 2 Cor. 3:18). Growth in holiness expressed through obedience, love, and virtue.

Stewardship (Generosity): Managing God's gifts—time, talent, and treasure—for His glory and others' good (1 Pet. 4:10; 2 Cor. 9:6–11). The opposite of hoarding; an act of worship.

Conviction: Spirit-born assurance that anchors belief and conduct in God's truth (John 16:8; Heb. 11:1). Turns doctrine into lived faith.

Hope: Confident expectation rooted in God's promises and Christ's resurrection (Rom. 5:1–5; 1 Pet. 1:3). Not wishful thinking but Easter realism.

Single–Mindedness: A heart undivided toward God (Matt. 6:22–24; James 1:8). Focused devotion that orders life around the Kingdom.

Communion (Abiding): Living union with Christ through Word, sacrament, and prayer (John

15:1–10). Alignment of will and love with the Father.

Treasures in Heaven: Imperishable riches—faith, hope, love, and the fruit of obedience (Matt. 6:19–21). The secure economy of the Kingdom.

Vocation: God's call to serve Him in all of life—home, church, marketplace (Col. 3:23–24). Work becomes worship and neighbor-love.

The Heart: The inner person—the wellspring of thought, desire, and action (Prov. 4:23; Matt. 12:35). God transforms the heart to transform the life.

Discernment (of Spirits): Testing what is true and from God (1 John 4:1; Phil. 1:9–10). Wisdom to choose the good and refuse the counterfeit.

Spiritual Gifts (Charisms): Holy Spirit endowments for building up the church (1 Cor. 12–14; Rom. 12:3–8; Eph. 4:7–13). Given for service, not status.

Spiritual Warfare: The believer's struggle against the powers of darkness, fought with the armor of God (Eph. 6:10–18); prayer, truth, righteousness, and the gospel of peace.

Angels and the Church: God's ministering spirits (Heb. 1:14) and the communion of saints (Heb. 12:1) by whom God often protects, guides, and encourages His people.

Communion of Saints (Great Cloud of Witnesses): The fellowship across time of all who are in

Christ—living and departed—united in worship and hope (Heb. 12:1; Rev. 7:9–12).

Guidance of the Holy Spirit: The Spirit leading God's people through Scripture, wise counsel, providence, and holy promptings (John 16:13; Acts 13:2).

Guarding the Heart (Armor of God): Practicing vigilance through prayer, Scripture, confession, and sacramental life (Prov. 4:23; Eph. 6:10–18).

Obedience: Loving submission to Christ's commands (John 14:15). Alignment of belief and behavior.

Peace of Christ: The settled shalom Jesus gives, not as the world gives (John 14:27; Phil. 4:6–7). Steadiness amid storms.

Perseverance: Enduring in faith through trial by God's grace (James 1:2–4; Rom. 5:3–5). Grit anchored in hope.

Victory in Christ: Christ's triumph over sin, death, and the devil (Col. 2:15; 1 Cor. 15:57). Believers share this victory through union with Him.

Notes

- Scripture quotations are taken from public-domain translations when possible (e.g., King James Version) or paraphrased in the author's words while preserving meaning and context.

- Historical and theological works cited above are recommended as guides that illuminate Scripture; where they differ, the Bible remains the final authority for faith and practice.

- Practices provided are intentionally simple, patterned after historic Christian disciplines (Acts 2:42)—Word, prayer, fellowship, sacramental life, generosity, and service.

- Readers are encouraged to test all things by Scripture (Acts 17:11), remain accountable within a local church, and pursue growth through prayer, mentoring, and faithful participation in the body of Christ.

ISBN 979-8-9993281-7-5

9 798999 328175

©2025 Woody R. Clermont. All rights reserved.

\

www.ingramcontent.com/pod-product-compliance
Lightning Source LLC
Chambersburg PA
CBHW071445090426
42737CB00011B/1785